99

BERLIOZ

FANTASTIC SYMPHONY

An Authoritative Score

Historical Background

Analysis · Views and Comments

NORTON CRITICAL SCORES

BACH **CANTATA NO. 4**
edited by Gerhard Herz

BACH **CANTATA NO. 140**
edited by Gerhard Herz

BEETHOVEN **SYMPHONY NO. 5 IN C MINOR**
edited by Elliot Forbes

BERLIOZ **FANTASTIC SYMPHONY**
edited by Edward T. Cone

CHOPIN **PRELUDES, OPUS 28**
edited by Thomas Higgins

DEBUSSY **PRELUDE TO "THE AFTERNOON OF A FAUN"**
edited by William W. Austin

MOZART **PIANO CONCERTO IN C MAJOR, K. 503**
edited by Joseph Kerman

MOZART **SYMPHONY IN G MINOR, K. 550**
edited by Nathan Broder

PALESTRINA **POPE MARCELLUS MASS**
edited by Lewis Lockwood

PURCELL **DIDO AND AENEAS**
edited by Curtis Price

SCHUBERT **SYMPHONY IN B MINOR ("UNFINISHED")**
edited by Martin Chusid

SCHUMANN **DICHTERLIEBE**
edited by Arthur Komar

STRAVINSKY **PETRUSHKA**
edited by Charles Hamm

WAGNER **PRELUDE AND TRANSFIGURATION**
from *TRISTAN AND ISOLDE*
edited by Robert Bailey

Hector Berlioz

FANTASTIC SYMPHONY

An Authoritative Score
Historical Background
Analysis   Views and Comments

Edited by

EDWARD T. CONE

PROFESSOR EMERITUS
PRINCETON UNIVERSITY

W · W · NORTON & COMPANY

New York · London

W. W. Norton & Company, Inc., 500 Fifth Avenue, New York, NY 10110
W. W. Norton & Company Ltd, 10 Coptic Street, London WC1A 1PU

Library of Congress Catalog Card No. 74-125861

ISBN 0-393-02160-2 Cloth Edition
ISBN 0-393-09926-1 Paper Edition

PRINTED IN THE UNITED STATES OF AMERICA

4 5 6 7 8 9 0

Contents

Preface   *vii*

The Historical Background
    The Composer and the Symphony   *3*
    The Symphony and the Program   *18*
    Hector Berlioz · On Imitation in Music   *36*

The Score of the Symphony
    1st Movement   *Rêveries. Passions*   *49*
    2nd Movement   *Un bal*   *81*
    3rd Movement   *Scène aux champs*   *106*
    4th Movement   *Marche au supplice*   *122*
    5th Movement   *Songe d'une nuit du sabbat*   *143*
    Textual Note   *197*

Analysis
    Two Contemporary Critiques
        François-Joseph Fétis · Critical Analysis   *215*
        Robert Schumann · A Symphony by Berlioz   *220*
    Edward T. Cone · Schumann Amplified: An Analysis   *249*

Views and Comments by Composers
    Felix Mendelssohn · [A Letter from Rome]   *281*
    Franz Liszt · A Berlioz Concert   *282*
    Richard Wagner · [On Berlioz and the Fantastic Symphony]   *284*
    Charles Gounod · [Berlioz]   *287*

Hugo Wolf · [On Berlioz and the Fantastic Symphony]   *289*
Camille Saint-Saëns · [The Fantastic Symphony]   *293*
Virgil Thomson · The Berlioz Case   *294*
Aaron Copland · Berlioz Today   *296*

And in Brief   *303*

Bibliography   *305*

Preface

The aim of this edition is twofold: to present an authentic score of the *Fantastic Symphony* and to surround it by documents that will enable the student to approach it both as a work of art and as an object of historical and critical study.

The first of these goals is difficult enough to achieve. Berlioz, although in many respects a meticulous orthographer, was not a very careful proofreader. Even after comparison of the manuscript with the first edition, puzzling details remain; all these are duly pointed out in the notes accompanying the score.

But it is easier to reconstruct the score than to find verbal accounts that, within a reasonable number of pages, give an adequate analytical, historical, and critical picture of the work. An unorthodox composition by a controversial composer, the *Fantastic Symphony* was bound to provoke a clash of contradictory opinions. What is remarkable is the extent to which Berlioz has remained controversial up to our own time. Although his champions may now seem to have carried the day, they nevertheless seem unwilling to let down their guard—no doubt with good reason.

One result of this kind of critical battle is a proliferation of polemical literature and a dearth of objective observation. It is hard to find sober reflection on a subject that has, at least once, driven respectable scholars to trading insults in the public press. In fact, I have come to the conclusion that it is impossible to approach the subject of Berlioz without bias. This being the case, it seemed to me that the most profitable set of prejudices to put before the reader would be the ones belonging to Berlioz himself and to those most intimately affected by what he did: his fellow-composers.

Accordingly, the early history of the *Fantastic Symphony* and the discussion of its program are told, so far as possible, in Berlioz's own words. My analysis is based on the famous essay by Schumann, here presented in its original unabridged version. But since this, in turn, was inspired as refutation of an article by Fétis, I have felt that I should do no less than Schumann himself did. He prefaced his own essay with a translation of the Fétis article; I have done the same.

The critical opinions are, I believe, a fair sample of those held by composers from Berlioz's day to the present. Some of them are familiar by now, but I hope that there will be a few surprises.

Specific acknowledgements for the use of copyrighted material are indicated in footnotes at the bottom of the appropriate pages; here I should like to record my thanks to a number of most helpful individuals. M. François Lesure of the Bibliothèque Nationale enabled me to use microfilms of the manuscript and early editions of the symphony in the collections of the Bibliothèque; this edition could not have been undertaken without his support. I am similarly indebted to Mr. Cecil Hopkinson, and to Miss Ruzena Wood of the National Library of Scotland, for making available to me films of the original orchestral parts. Miss Paula Morgan of the Princeton University Library and Mr. Thor Wood of the Lincoln Center Library of the Performing Arts showed unfailing personal interest in this project, which made it a pleasure to work with the music collections of the two libraries. Professors Leon-François Hoffmann and Walter Kaufmann very kindly answered my questions about the French and German translations respectively. I owe it to them that errors are not more numerous than they are; those that remain are entirely my own responsibility. For various favors, points of information, bits of advice, and good common sense, I wish to thank Messrs. Bernard Herrmann and Virgil Thomson, and Professors Paul Henry Lang, Arthur Mendel, and Gregory Vlastos. And finally I should like to indicate my gratitude to Mr. David Hamilton, of W. W. Norton & Company, for persuading me to undertake what turned out to be an engrossing task.

EDWARD T. CONE

THE HISTORICAL
BACKGROUND

The Composer and the Symphony

Saint-Saëns called Hector Berlioz a paradox in human form.[1] The phrase has been much quoted, and with approval; but Berlioz was in fact an unusually consistent example of the self-conscious and articulate artistic genius of the nineteenth century. He was self-conscious in his early recognition of his own musical talent and in his determination to foster it; he was articulate in his use of words—explanations, appreciations, criticisms, excoriations—to complement his music in support of what he took to be his cultural mission. What this was can be very succinctly stated: he took music seriously, and he wanted others to take it seriously. And so he found himself in constant battle against the academics of the Paris Conservatory, for whom music was an exercise in the application of memorized rules; against a French musical culture so narrow in outlook and restricted in esthetic that it had not yet fully accepted Beethoven; against performers who refused to follow the composer's explicit directions; against the kind of conductor who could pause at a crucial point to take a pinch of snuff[2]; and against a public that tolerated all this with indifference because it considered music to be a mere form of entertainment. For Berlioz, music was the dramatic expression of an emotional experience, an imitation of life itself.

But Berlioz, though serious, was not solemn; and this may be one reason why Saint-Saëns found him full of paradox. Much of his prose is couched in a witty style that makes generous use of irony, even of self-

1. "Un paradoxe fait homme," the opening phrase of the essay on Berlioz in Camille Saint-Saëns, *Portraits et Souvenirs*, Paris, 1899, p. 3.

2. See the famous anecdote in *The Memoirs of Hector Berlioz*, transl. by David Cairns, New York, 1969, p. 231. This and all other references to the *Memoirs* (unless otherwise stated) apply to the English translation by David Cairns. All quoted material reprinted by permission of Alfred A. Knopf, Inc., and David Cairns.

chastising romantic irony. Like his music, it abounds in startling juxta-positions of contrasting ideas, and in exaggerations both humorous and dramatic. As a result, Berlioz's writings are much more readable, and they reveal a much more sympathetic character behind them, than those of another Great Romantic Composer with a Mission: Richard Wagner. More than that, they exhibit yet another facet of the consistency of Berlioz's personality: his constant view of his own life as an absorbing drama, of which he was the hero. One might better say that these writings betray his constant attempt to live as the hero of a drama. In what follows, therefore, I have tried so far as possible to let the composer tell the story of the writing of the *Fantastic Symphony* in his own words.

Our history begins in the village of Meylan, near Grenoble—and not very far from La Côte Saint-André, where Hector-Louis Berlioz was born in 1803, the son of a small-town doctor. It was to Meylan that Mme. Berlioz took her children each summer to visit their grandfather. And it was here that the youthful Hector first encountered romantic love—at the age of twelve.

In the highest part of Meylan, right against the mountainside, is a small white house half hidden in gardens and vineyards with a wide prospect over the valley of the Isère far below; behind, a few craggy hillocks, an old tower in ruins, a wood, and the commanding bulk of the great rock-bastion of Saint-Eynard: in fact a spot clearly marked out to be the scene of some romantic drama. It was the villa of Madame Gautier. She lived there during the summer with her two nieces, the younger of whom was called Estelle. The name alone would have been enough to arouse my interest. It was already dear to me from Florian's pastorale *Estelle et Némorin*,[3] which I had discovered in my father's library and secretly read and re-read a hundred times. This Estelle, however, was a girl of eighteen with a tall, elegant figure, large eyes ready primed for the attack (though they were always smiling), a head of hair that would have graced Achilles' helmet, and the feet, I will not say of an Andalusian, but of a pure-bred Parisian. And she wore pink half-boots. I had never seen such things before. You may laugh; but although I have forgotten the colour of her hair (I believe it was black), I cannot think of her without seeing before me, dazzling as those great eyes of hers, the little pink boots.

The moment I beheld her, I was conscious of an electric shock: I loved her. From then on I lived in a daze. I hoped for nothing, I knew nothing, yet my heart felt weighed down by an immense sadness. I lay awake whole nights disconsolate. By day I hid myself in the maize fields or in the secret corners of my grandfather's orchard, like a wounded

3. Jean Pierre Claris de Florian (1755-94) was a well-known writer of plays and romances. Berlioz's favorite work appeared in 1788.

bird, mute, suffering. Jealousy plagued me, pale companion of all true lovers. The least word addressed by any man to my divinity was torture to me. I can still hear—with the same shudder—the ring of my uncle's spurs as he danced with her. Everyone at home and in the neighborhood laughed at the spectacle of a child of twelve broken on the wheel of a love beyond his years. She herself, who had been the first to realize the truth, was much amused, I am sure.[4]

The relationship, such as it was, lasted only briefly. But years later, when Berlioz was thirty, a passing encounter convinced him that he was still in love with her. In a strange way, perhaps he was—indeed, was all his life. Thus in 1848, hearing that Estelle Fornier, *née* Duboeuf, was widowed and living near Meylan, he made an abortive effort to see her; but it was not until 1864, when he was sixty, that he succeeded. By this time he himself was twice widowed, ill, and prematurely aging. His renewed friendship with Estelle sustained him through his last difficult years (he died in 1869), and provided a suitably romantic ending for his *Memoirs,* which close with an account of the reunion.

This story reveals many of the leading motives of Berlioz's life. The infatuation at first sight, the hopeless longing for the "Unattainable One," the ideal of space-defying and time-conquering love: these are all recurring themes in the composer's life. Especially characteristic, too, is the apparent literary inspiration behind the whole affair: the young Berlioz's self-identification with the hero of Florian's pastorale. Equally typical, and still more important, is the way the young musician's emotional state stimulated his efforts at composition; and it is here that we find the germ of the *Fantastic Symphony.*

My youthful essays in composition bore the stamp of a profound melancholy. Almost all my melodies were in the minor. I was aware of this limitation but could not help it. My romantic Meylan passion had edged my thoughts in a permanent black crêpe. In this state of soul, reading *Estelle et Némorin* ceaselessly, it was not unlikely that I would end by setting to music some of its many ditties whose watery charms I then found sweet. And sure enough I did.

I wrote, among others, one intensely sad song to words which expressed my despair at leaving the woods and the haunts which had been "graced by the footsteps and lighted by the eyes",[5] and by the pink boots, of my cruel fair one. The pale verses come back to me now in a shaft of spring sunshine, as I sit here in London, preoccupied with

4. *Memoirs,* pp. 36–37.
5. "Honorés par les pas, éclairés par les yeux," from La Fontaine's fable *Les Deux pigeons.*

urgent affairs, racked by anxieties, raging at the absurd obstacles which beset me here as elsewhere. I quote the first stanza:

> Je vais donc quitter pour jamais
> Mon doux pays, ma douce amie.
> Loin d'eux je vais traîner ma vie
> Dans les pleurs et dans les regrets!
> Fleuve dont j'ai vu l'eau limpide,
> Pour réfléchir ses doux attraits,
> Suspendre sa course rapide,
> Je vais vous quitter pour jamais.

As for the tune of this romance (which, along with the sextet and the quintets, I burnt before leaving for Paris), it presented itself humbly before my mind when I began to write my Fantastic Symphony in 1829. It seemed to me exactly right for expressing the overpowering sadness of a young heart first caught in the toils of a hopeless love, and I welcomed it. It is the theme played by the first violins at the beginning of the largo in the opening movement of the work, Reverie: Passion. I put it in unchanged.[6]

The scene now shifts to Paris, where Berlioz, after finding himself temperamentally unable to pursue the medical career his father had planned for him, turned irrevocably to music. He studied counterpoint and composition at the Conservatory and produced his first large-scale works. These were received, for the most part, with the amazed incomprehension that was to become the standard reaction to each of Berlioz's new productions. But the crucial event of those years, which occurred on September 11, 1827, was not a musical one.

I come now to the supreme drama of my life. I shall not recount all its sad vicissitudes. I will say only this: an English company came over to Paris to give a season of Shakespeare at the Odéon, with a repertory of plays then quite unknown in France. I was at the first night of *Hamlet*. In the role of Ophelia I saw Henriette Smithson, who five years later became my wife. The impression made on my heart and mind by

6. *Memoirs*, pp. 41–42. The melody referred to is to be found at the beginning of the symphony (I, mm. 3–16). The stanza, which is taken from *Estelle et Némorin*, may be translated:

> Forever, then, shall I forsake
> Beloved home, beloved friend.
> Far, far from them my life I'll spend
> In tears, with heart's regretful ache!
> O river, whose clear stream I've seen
> Pause in its rapid course to make
> A mirror for her lovely mien,
> You, too, forever I forsake.

her extraordinary talent, nay her dramatic genius, was equalled only by
the havoc wrought in me by the poet she so nobly interpreted. That is
all I can say.[7]

One cannot fail to note the resemblances here to the Estelle affair.
There is the same literary inspiration, the same love at first sight, the
same apparently hopeless attachment. Harriet Smithson (that was her
real name, although Berlioz always called her Henriette) was an Anglo-
Irish actress (1800–54) then at the height of her success. She did not
even know of her admirer's existence. In fact, much of Berlioz's musical
and personal activity during the next months was designed to bring his
name to her attention. In this he achieved only limited success. She did
learn of the young musician and received letters from him; but when she
left Paris in 1829 the two had never met.

Berlioz, undaunted, continued to nourish his passion. To Humbert
Ferrand (d. 1805–68), a young poet who had become Berlioz's close friend
and constant correspondent, he wrote on February 6, 1830:

> After a period of calm violently disturbed by the composition of
> the *Élégie en prose,* which is the last of my Songs, I have just been
> plunged again into all the tortures of an endless and unquenchable pas-
> sion, without cause, without purpose. She is still in London, and yet I
> seem to feel her around me; I hear my heart pounding, and its beats set
> me going like the piston strokes of a steam engine. Each muscle of my
> body trembles with pain.—Useless!—Frightening!—
>
> Oh! Unhappy woman! If she could for one moment conceive all the
> poetry, all the infinity of such a love, she would fly to my arms, even if
> she must die from my embrace.
>
> I was on the point of beginning my grand symphony (*Episode from
> the Life of an Artist*), in which the development of my infernal passion
> is to be depicted; I have it all in my head, but I can write nothing. Let's
> wait.[8]

It was at this point that Berlioz heard, and for a time believed, mali-
cious gossip connecting Miss Smithson with her manager. This was a
painful blow, but it brought him to his senses—and enabled him to continue the composition of his symphony. His disillusionment with his
beloved apparently had a decisive effect on the final form of the work.
On April 16 he wrote to Ferrand:

> . . . since my last letter, I have gone through some terrible squalls, my
> ship has cracked up badly, but it has at last righted itself; now it sails

7. *Memoirs*, p. 95.
8. Hector Berlioz, *Lettres intimes*, Paris, 1882, pp. 63–64. This letter and those
that follow are translated by the editor.

fairly well. Frightful facts, whose truth I cannot doubt, have started me toward a cure; and I believe that it will be as complete as my tenacious spirit can allow. I have just confirmed my resolution by a work that satisfies me completely. Here is its subject, which will be published in a program and distributed in the hall on the day of the concert.

Episode from the Life of an Artist (grand fantastic symphony in five parts) .

FIRST MOVEMENT: double, made up of a short adagio, immediately followed by a fully developed allegro (*vague des passions*,[9] aimless reveries; frenzied passion with all its fits of tenderness, jealousy, fury, fears, etc., etc.) .

SECOND MOVEMENT: *Scene in the Country* (adagio, thoughts of love and hope troubled by dark presentiments) .

THIRD MOVEMENT: *A Ball* (brilliant and stirring music) .

FOURTH MOVEMENT: March to the Scaffold (fierce, pompous music) .

FIFTH MOVEMENT: *Dream of a Witches' Sabbath.*

Now, my friend, here is how I have put together my novel, or rather my tale, whose hero you will have no difficulty in recognizing.

I imagine that an artist, gifted with a vivid imagination, finding himself in that state of mind that Chateaubriand has depicted so admirably in *René*,[10] sees for the first time a woman who embodies the ideal of beauty and fascination that his heart has long been seeking; he falls desperately in love with her. As the result of an odd whim, whenever the image of the loved one appears before his mind's eye it is accompanied by a musical thought in whose character he finds a grace and a nobility akin to those he attributes to his beloved. This double *idée fixe* pursues him incessantly: that is the reason for the constant appearance, in every movement of the symphony, of the chief melody of the first allegro (No. 1) .

After periods of great agitation, he begins to entertain hope; he believes that his love is returned. Finding himself one day in the country, he hears in the distance two shepherds piping a *ranz des vaches*[11] in dialogue; this pastorale immerses him in a delightful reverie (No. 2) . The principal melody reappears for a moment against the motifs of the adagio.

9. An almost untranslatable phrase coined by (François René, Vicomte de) Chateaubriand (1768–1848) , who was one of the seminal influences of the romantic movement in French literature. By "le vague des passions" he meant aimlessness of passion, emotional uncertainty—the state of mind in which one experiences passionate emotions of great intensity, yet without any definite object. It is especially characteristic of young people emerging from adolescence, aware of their great emotional potential yet vague as to its proper direction. See Jacques Barzun, *Berlioz and the Romantic Century*, 3rd ed., New York, 1969, I, 162-63.

10. One of the author's best-known works. It first appeared as a semifictional episode in *La Génie du christianisme* (1802) , but was later published separately.

11. A kind of melody, typically played on the alphorn, used by herdsmen in the mountains to call their cows.

He goes to a ball, but the uproar of the party fails to distract him; his *idée fixe* returns to trouble him, and the beloved melody makes his heart pound during a brilliant waltz (No. 3).

In a fit of despair, he poisons himself with opium; but, instead of killing him, the narcotic induces a horrible vision. In the course of it he believes that he has killed his beloved, has been condemned to death, and witnesses his own execution. March to the scaffold; a huge procession of headsmen, soldiers, populace. At the end, the *melody* reappears once more, like a last thought of love, interrupted by the fatal blow (No. 4).

He sees himself surrounded by a foul assembly of sorcerers and devils, come together to celebrate the sabbath. They call afar. At last the *melody* arrives. Hitherto it had appeared only in graceful form, but now it has become a vulgar tune, trivial and mean; it is the loved one coming to the sabbath to attend the funeral procession of her victim. She is now only a prostitute, fit to take part in such an orgy. Then the ceremony begins. The bells ring, the whole infernal crew prostrate themselves, a chorus sings the plainchant sequence of the dead (*Dies irae*), two other choruses repeat it, parodying it in burlesque fashion. Then finally the sabbath round-dance begins to whirl; in its most violent outburst, it mingles with the *Dies irae*, and the dream is over (No. 5).

There, my friend, is the sketch of what I have done in this huge symphony. I have just written the last note. If I can be ready on Whitsunday, May 30, I shall give a concert at the Nouveautés[12] with an orchestra of two hundred and twenty musicians. I'm afraid I won't be able to get the parts copied. Right now I'm a dolt; the frightful mental effort that produced my work has tired out my imagination, and I wish I could spend all my time sleeping and resting. But, if the brain sleeps, the heart is wakeful, and I am acutely aware of missing you. Oh, my friend, shan't I be seeing you again?[13]

Such was Berlioz's first disclosure of the plan of his symphony, his first statement of its program. Except for the details of the pastorale and its position before the waltz (the two were soon to be reversed), the outline is substantially the one familiar to us today.

A few weeks later, as if afraid that his friend might take amiss his symbolically brutal treatment of Miss Smithson through the parody of her musical counterpart, he wrote (May 13):

My revenge is not too severe. Besides, it wasn't in that spirit that I wrote the *Dream of a Witches' Sabbath*. I don't want to take revenge. I pity her and despise her. She is an ordinary woman, gifted with an instinctive

12. Théâtre des Nouveautés, a Parisian theater that specialized in musical productions.

13. *Lettres intimes*, pp. 65–69.

genius for expressing lacerations of the human soul that she has never felt, and incapable of conceiving a great and noble passion such as mine for her.[14]

It is interesting to contrast these outpourings with the account of the same period that Berlioz gave in his *Memoirs*, written over twenty years later. Here are no reference to personal suffering, no mention of the calumny against Miss Smithson (which had, by this time, long been discredited). Instead, the composer reveals a literary source of inspiration: Goethe's *Faust*, which he was reading in French translation. The immediate musical result of this encounter was a kind of cantata entitled *Eight Scenes from Faust*; its ultimate fruit, much later, was the "dramatic legend" *The Damnation of Faust*. But Berlioz insists that the *Fantastic Symphony*, too, had its connections with Goethe's play.

> Immediately after the composition of the *Faust* pieces, and still under the influence of Goethe's poem, I wrote my Fantastic Symphony: very slowly and laboriously in some parts, with extraordinary ease in others. The adagio (the Scene in the Country), which always affects the public and myself so keenly, cost me nearly a month's arduous toil; two or three times I gave it up. On the other hand, the March to the Scaffold was written in a night. But I continued to make considerable changes to both movements, and to the rest of the work, over the course of several years.[15]

Certain critics, notably Tom S. Wotton,[16] have deduced, from very flimsy premises, a much closer relationship between *Faust* and the symphony. Berlioz had been working not only on songs from the play but also on a ballet on the subject, which he hoped would be accepted by the Paris Opera. It never was, and the music, at least in that form, has not survived; but some of it may have been preserved in the *Ball* and the *Witches' Sabbath*. Ernest Newman[17] wants to find the origin of the Pastorale there too. Wotton suggests that this movement came from *Les Francs-juges*, an unfinished opera of the same period.

All this is pure speculation. More serious, because based on evidence—controversial, to be sure—in the manuscript, is Adolphe Boschot's insistence that the entire *March to the Scaffold* was lifted, almost verbatim, from the same opera, where it served as a "March of the Guard."[18] This charge touched off a furious debate between Boschot and

14. *Ibid.*, p. 70.
15. *Memoirs*, p. 126.
16. *Berlioz: Four Works*, London, 1929, pp. 5–6.
17. See his edition of the *Memoirs*, New York, 1932, p. 98, n. 1.
18. *La Jeunesse d'un romantique*, Paris, 1906, pp. 393–94.

Berlioz's staunch defender Julien Tiersot.[19] For a long time the question remained unsettled. Barzun, for example, found the evidence "inconclusive."[20] But a fresh look at the autographs of the symphony and of surviving fragments of the opera has recently led Hugh Macdonald to make a watertight case for Boschot's attribution (although not for Boschot's refusal to accept Berlioz's claim to have written the *March* in a single night) .[21]

Certainly Berlioz did not hesitate to borrow from himself. We have already seen one example of this in his use of the "Estelle" theme in the opening Largo. Another case is the *idée fixe*: this was taken from a cantata, *Herminie*, written in 1828 in an unsuccessful effort to obtain the Prix de Rome. But there seems to be no justification for the view that the whole symphony was a hodgepodge put together from whatever used goods, leftovers, and scraps the composer found at hand. The unity of the symphony, which, as our analysis will later try to show, goes much deeper than the mere recurrence of the *idée fixe*, speaks out clearly against such a verdict.

To return to our narrative: the first scheduled performance of the symphony proved to be abortive. The Théâtre des Nouveautés turned out to be ill-equipped for such an undertaking. Berlioz's hundred and thirty musicians, even though a considerably smaller number than his hoped-for two hundred and twenty, were too many for the resources of the hall. It was not until the following winter that the symphony received its première.

The intervening months had been eventful ones for the composer. He had fallen in love again, this time with Camille Moke (1811–75) , a young pianist who apparently mingled virtuosity and personal charm in equal measure. For once Berlioz had chosen an approachable object, one who encouraged his attentions. (She was evidently all too approachable, and not only by Berlioz.) For this reason, when he was finally awarded the coveted Prix de Rome that October, he was not as pleased as he might have been: he had to leave Paris and his new beloved. Before going, however, he wished to present to the public both his prize-winning cantata, *Sardanapalus*, and the *Fantastic Symphony*.

   . . . I organized a concert at the Conservatoire at which the academic offering figured along with the Fantastic Symphony, a work that had not

   19. See *Le Ménestrel, passim,* May 20–Aug. 5, 1906.
   20. *Op. cit.,* I, 160, n. 23.
   21. "Hector Berlioz 1969—A Centenary Assessment," *Adam,* Nos. 331–33, 1969, pp. 35–47.

yet been heard. Habeneck[22] undertook to conduct and all the players, with a generosity for which I shall always be profoundly grateful, for the third time gave their services.

On the day before the concert, Liszt called on me. It was our first meeting. I spoke of Goethe's *Faust*, which he confessed that he had not read, but which he soon came to love as much as I. We felt an immediate affinity, and from that moment our friendship has grown ever closer and stronger. He came to the concert and was conspicuous for the warmth of his applause and his generally enthusiastic behaviour.

The performance was by no means perfect—it hardly could be, with works of such difficulty and after only two rehearsals. But it was good enough to give a reasonable idea of the music. Three of the movements of the symphony, the Waltz, the March to the Scaffold and the Witches' Sabbath, created a sensation; the March especially took the audience by storm. The Scene in the Country made no impression at all. But it bore little resemblance to the present version. I made up my mind at once to rewrite it. Ferdinand Hiller,[23] who was then in Paris, gave me some excellent advice which I endeavoured to profit by.

The cantata was well performed; the conflagration caught fire at the appointed time, the palace crashed in ruins. Altogether it was a great success. A few days later the watchdogs of the Press pronounced their verdicts, some for, some against, both equally vehement. The hostile critics nearly all blamed me for the wrong things. Instead of pointing out the palpable defects in both works—serious defects which in the case of the symphony it took me several years of the most diligent labour to expunge—they attacked the absurd ideas I was supposed to have, though I had never had them, the crudeness of certain modulations which were not there at all, the systematic failure to observe certain fundamental rules of music which I had faithfully observed, and the neglect of certain musical procedures which I had employed precisely in those passages where their absence was deplored. I must confess my partisans too have often been given to crediting me with ridiculous and totally alien intentions. The amount of fatuous theorizing and sheer foolishness poured forth by French critics in praise as well as execration of my music since that time beggars description. Two or three men at the most had the sense and intelligence, when I appeared on the scene, to reserve judgment and write about me with moderation. But critics who are both knowledgeable and perceptive, who combine imagination, sensitivity and an unprejudiced mind and are capable of assessing me sanely and of understanding what I am aiming at, are few and far between even now. In the early years of my career they did not exist at all; and even had they existed, the rare and far from expert performances

22. François-Antoine Habeneck (1781–1849), the snuff-taking conductor, who was nevertheless one of the best in Paris at the time.

23. Ferdinand Hiller (1811–85), German pianist, conductor, and composer. He was a good friend of Berlioz and, later, of Mendelssohn.

of my works to be heard then would have left a great deal to their imaginations.[24]

December 5, 1830, was the date, and it is an important one. It marked the end of Berlioz's apprenticeship and the beginning of his career as a professional composer, and it vividly brought to the attention of the public the fact that it was entering a new musical era. For despite the many traditional and even eclectic elements of the symphony, despite its obeisance to classical formal procedures, despite the composer's insistence on his harmonic orthodoxy, this music *sounded* like no music ever before heard. The proof of its great originality is that today, almost a century and a half later, it still sounds like no other music; and not very long ago critics were still attacking it for its disregard of accepted procedures.[25]

Probably most of the audience at that historic concert failed to grasp Berlioz's harmonic boldness and melodic freshness, or were put off by them; but even they must have realized that the composer was using the orchestra in a new way. Not only was he assigning quasi-dramatic roles to one instrument or section after another, but he was assembling, from the orchestral ensemble as a whole, one huge virtuoso instrument—much as Chopin (to pursue a comparison suggested by Schumann) created his new sound by emphasizing both the individual character of the piano's various melodic ranges and the harmonic unification of the entire keyboard by the use of the pedal. Berlioz's sound has been in the ears of composers ever since, even when they have reacted most strongly against it. And though refined in his later works, it is present in every essential in the *Fantastic Symphony*. As Barzun says, "It is through that work that he first became known, and from it one can date his unremitting influence on nineteenth-century composers."[26]

Berlioz went to Rome, and one of the labors that occupied him during his residence at the Academy was his revision of the symphony, especially the *Scene in the Country* and the *Ball*. While he was working on the latter he heard appalling news about Mlle. Moke, now (so he thought) his fiancée. This time it was no calumny: she was indeed marrying Camille Pleyel, the pianist and piano maker. The news plunged Berlioz into a fit of desperation that precipitated one of the most ludi-

24. *Memoirs*, pp. 139–40.

25. See, for example, Donald Francis Tovey, *Essays in Musical Analysis*, London, 1939, VI, 44–50.

26. *Op. cit.*, p. 151.

crous escapades of his life. The story is too long to relate here, but it is too good to miss: it can be found in Chapter 34 of the *Memoirs*.[27]

He was also compiling and completing the strange mélange eventually to be called *Lélio, or the Return to Life*. This was designed as a sequel to the symphony, constituting Part II of the *Episode from the Life of an Artist*. It was to be staged as a *mélologue,* or musical monodrama— a playlet whose single character, the reawakening artist, evokes through his memories and fantasies the various movements of the work. Eager to arrange a performance at which the revised symphony and its companion piece could be heard together, Berlioz obtained permission to leave Rome before his two-year term had elapsed. After a few months at home he returned to Paris in November, 1832.

What happened then is again best told in his own words.

My old apartment in the rue Richelieu where I lived before going to Rome had, I discovered, been let. Some impulse moved me to take rooms in the house opposite, 1 rue Neuve-Saint-Marc, which Miss Smithson had at one time occupied. Next day, meeting the old servant who had for many years been housekeeper to the establishment, I asked what had become of Miss Smithson and whether she had heard any news of her. "But sir, didn't you . . . She's in Paris, she was staying here only a few days ago. She left the day before yesterday and moved to the rue de Rivoli. She was in the apartment that you have now. She is director of an English company that's opening next week." I stood aghast at the extraordinary series of coincidences. It was fate. I saw it was no longer possible for me to struggle against it. For two years I had heard nothing of the fair Ophelia; I had had no idea where she was, whether in England, Scotland or America; and here I was, arriving from Italy at exactly the moment when she reappeared after a tour of northern Europe. We had just missed meeting each other in the same house; I had taken the apartment that she had left the previous evening.

A believer in the magnetic attractions and secret affinities of the heart would find in all this some fine arguments to support his theories. Without going so far, I reasoned as follows: I had come to Paris to have my new work (the monodrama) performed. If I went to the English theatre and saw her again before I had given my concert, the old delirium tremens would inevitably seize me. As before, I would lose all independence of will and be incapable of the attention and concentrated effort which the enterprise demanded. Let me first give my concert. Afterwards I would see her, whether as Ophelia or as Juliet, even if it killed me; I would give myself up to the destiny which seemed to pursue me, and not struggle any more.

27. Pp. 152–58. Pleyel (1788–1855) soon regretted the marriage. See *Memoirs,* pp. 553–54, note on Camille Moke.

Therefore, though the dread Shakespearean names beckoned to me daily from the walls of Paris, I resisted their blandishments and the concert was arranged.

The programme consisted of my Fantastic Symphony followed by its sequel *Lélio* or *The Return to Life*, the monodrama which forms the second part of the "Episode in the Life of an Artist." The subject of this musical drama, as is known, was none other than my love for Miss Smithson and the anguish and "bad dreams" it had brought me. Now consider the incredible chain of accidents which follows.

Two days before the concert—which I thought of as a farewell to art and life—I was in Schlesinger's music shop[28] when an Englishman came in and almost immediately went out again. "Who was that?" I asked Schlesinger, moved by a curiosity for which there was no rational motive. "That's Schutter, who writes for *Galignani's Messenger*. Wait a moment," he added, striking his forehead, "I have an idea. Let me have a box for your concert. Schutter knows Miss Smithson. I'll ask him to take her the tickets and persuade her to come." The suggestion made me shudder, but I lacked the strength of mind to reject it. I gave him the tickets. Schlesinger ran after Schutter, caught him up, and doubtless explained what a stir the presence of the famous actress would create. Schutter promised to do everything he could to get her there.

While I was occupied with rehearsals and all the other preparations, the unfortunate director of the English company was busy ruining herself. The guileless actress had been counting on the continued enthusiasm of the Parisians and on the support of the new school of writers who three years earlier had lauded both Shakespeare and his interpreter to the skies. But Shakespeare was no longer a novelty to the feckless and frivolous public. The literary revolution demanded by the romantics had been achieved; and not only were the leaders of the movement not eager for any further demonstration of the power of the greatest of all dramatic poets: unconsciously, they feared it. It was not in their interests that the public should become too familiar with works from which they had borrowed so extensively.

The result was that the English company excited little response, and receipts were low. It had been an expensive venture. The season showed a deficit which absorbed the imprudent director's entire capital. This was the situation when Schutter called on Miss Smithson and offered her a box for my concert, and this is what ensued. She herself told me long afterwards.

Schutter found her in a state of profound despondency, and his proposal was at first badly received. At such a moment it was hardly to be expected she should have time for music. But Miss Smithson's sister joined with him in urging her to accept: it would be a distraction for her; and an English actor, who was with them, on his side appeared anxious to take advantage of the offer. A cab was summoned, and Miss

28. Maurice Schlesinger (1798–1871), who was to publish the *Fantastic Symphony*.

Smithson allowed herself, half willingly, half forcibly, to be escorted into it. The triumphant Schutter gave the address: "The Conservatoire," and they were off. On the way the unhappy creature glanced at the programme. My name had not been mentioned. She now learnt that I was the originator of the proceedings. The title of the symphony and the headings of the various movements somewhat astonished her; but it never so much as occurred to her that the heroine of this strange and doleful drama might be herself.

On entering the stage box above a sea of musicians (for I had collected a very large orchestra), she was aware of a buzz of interest all over the hall. Everyone seemed to be staring in her direction; a thrill of emotion went through her, half excitement, half fear, which she could not clearly account for. Habeneck was conducting. When I came in and sat breathlessly down behind him, Miss Smithson, who until then had supposed she might have mistaken the name at the head of the programme, recognized me. "Yes, it is he," she murmured; "poor young man, I expect he has forgotten me; at least . . . I hope he has." The symphony began and produced a tremendous effect. (Those were days when the hall of the Conservatoire, from which I am now excluded, was the focus of immense public enthusiasm.) The brilliant reception, the passionate character of the work, its ardent, exalted melodies, its protestations of love, its sudden outbursts of violence, and the sensation of hearing an orchestra of that size close to, could not fail to make an impression—an impression as profound as it was totally unexpected—on her nervous system and poetic imagination, and in her heart of hearts she thought, "Ah, if he still loved me!" During the interval which followed the performance of the symphony, the ambiguous remarks of Schutter, and of Schlesinger too—for he had been unable to resist coming into her box—and their veiled allusions to the cause of this young composer's well-known troubles of the heart, began to make her suspect the truth, and she heard them in growing agitation. But when Bocage,[29] the actor who spoke the part of Lélio (that is, myself), declaimed these lines:

> Oh, if I could only find her, the Juliet, the Ophelia whom my heart cries out for! If I could drink deep of the mingled joy and sadness that real love offers us, and one autumn evening on some wild heath with the north wind blowing over it, lie in her arms and sleep a last, long, sorrowful sleep!

"God!" she thought: "Juliet—Ophelia! Am I dreaming? I can no longer doubt. It is of me he speaks. He loves me still." From that moment, so she has often told me, she felt the room reel about her; she heard no more but sat in a dream, and at the end returned home like a sleepwalker, with no clear notion of what was happening.

The date was 9th December 1832.[30]

29. The stage name of Pierre-Martinien Tousez (1797–1863), a popular actor of the day.

30. *Memoirs*, pp. 214–17.

It must be remembered that even now Miss Smithson had never actually met her distant suitor! That confrontation finally took place the next day. From then on events moved quickly. The two were married the following fall.

Within a few years they were miserable. They were formally separated in 1844, and Harriet died in 1854. The same year Berlioz married Marie Recio (1814–62), a singer who had long been his mistress; he was not happy with her either. But these depressing events are not really germane to our narrative. The early history of the *Fantastic Symphony* should end on October 3, 1833, the wedding day of Hector Berlioz and his Henriette, with the hope that the two live happily ever after.

The Symphony and the Program

The relationship between the program and the music of the *Fantastic Symphony* has been the source of as much discussion and controversy as the music itself. Is a familiarity with the program necessary to an understanding of the music? Or is it actually detrimental to the musical experience? Is the symphony viable as absolute music? Did Berlioz write the music to fit the program or vice versa? And so on.

Certainly the program was one element—perhaps the chief element—that captured the imagination of the contemporary public. It was not so much the mere existence of the accompanying story—the device was already common enough in those days—as its sensational nature, with its suggestions of mingled sexuality and diabolism. But should one go so far as to conclude, with Barzun, that it can be "relegated . . . to the role of promotional aid"?[1] Or should one accept Hugh Macdonald's opposite point of view, that "it is a fashionable analytical folly that urges us to consider the work as 'pure music' "?[2] Perhaps the correct point of view is somewhere between the two: "With Berlioz the programme was often as much a matter of inspiration as the music itself. As a rule, the music was composed first, and an appropriate title found afterward."[3]

One reason for this diversity of opinion is that Berlioz's own position on program music underwent modification over the years. This development can be traced, first in a series of documents relating specifically to the *Fantastic Symphony*, and then in an essay on the subject in general that the composer published in 1837.

1. *Berlioz and the Romantic Century*, 3rd ed., New York, 1969, I, 162.
2. From the jacket of the recording by Ernest Ansermet and the Orchestre de la Suisse Romande, London Records Inc., CSA 2101.
3. Tom S. Wotton, *Berlioz: Four Works*, London, 1929, p. 5.

The proper title of the symphony, according to the manuscript and the announcements of the first performance, is *Épisode de la vie d'un artiste, Symphonie fantastique en cinq parties*. This order is preserved in the first printed edition (Paris: Maurice Schlesinger, 1845; the work is here given an opus number, 14, and dedicated to Czar Nicholas I of Russia). The important point is that the composer evidently considered the formal description *Symphonie fantastique* as a mere subtitle. But at least one later printing of substantially the same edition (Paris: G. Brandus & S. Dufour), which Cecil Hopkinson places "after 1858,"[4] reverses title and subtitle; *Symphonie fantastique, Première partie de l'Épisode de la vie d'un artiste, oeuvre lyrique* is now the complete heading. Berlioz probably chose this new wording and in any case almost certainly approved it, since a copy of this printing in the Bibliothèque Nationale contains notes and corrections in the master's own hand. The title reflects the connection of the symphony with its sequel, *Lélio* (since it is now only "Part One of the Episode"); but, since the word *Symphonie* so conspicuously predominates in the new typographical layout, the reversal may also indicate the composer's altered attitude toward the importance of his program—of which more later.

The title page of the manuscript (also in the Bibliothèque Nationale) contains two epigraphs that Berlioz may once have intended to appear in the published edition, although neither was ever so used. Like the reference to Chateaubriand to be embodied, as we shall see, in the program, these show Berlioz adducing literary parallels for the state of mind he wished to convey musically. The shorter of the two is a French translation of the familiar lines from *King Lear* (IV, 1):

> Like flies to wanton boys are we to the gods:
> They kill us for their sport.

The other is a lengthy quotation from the first poem of Victor Hugo's *Feuilles d'automne*. This was published in 1831, so the quotation could hardly have been attached to the symphony before the period of its revision in Rome. The same lines appeared as an epigraph to the libretto of *Lélio* when it was published in 1832:

> Certes, plus d'un vieillard, sans flamme, sans cheveux,
> Tombé de lassitude au bout de tous ses voeux,
> · Pâlirait s'il voyait, comme un gouffre dans l'onde,
> Mon âme où ma pensée habite comme un monde,

4. *A Bibliography of the Musical and Literary Works of Hector Berlioz 1803–69*, Edinburgh, 1951, p. 76, No. 36-B (d).

Tout ce que j'ai souffert, tout ce que j'ai tenté,
Tout ce qui m'a menti comme un fruit avorté,
Mon plus beau temps passé sans espoir qu'il renaisse,
Les amours, les travaux, les deuils de ma jeunesse,
Et quoiqu'encor a l'âge où l'avenir sourit,
Le livre de mon coeur à toute page écrit.

These gloomy sentiments may be approximated in English blank verse thus:

Sure, more than one old man, burnt out and bald,
Reduced through weariness to desiring naught,
Would blanch could he but see my whirlpool soul,
The world wherein my thought has found its home,
All I have suffered, all I have essayed,
All that's deluded me like stunted fruit,
My best of life gone, never to return,
The labors, loves, and sorrows of my youth,
And, though the future smile on one my age,
My heart's book written out on every page.

The headings of the five movements in the autograph accord with the plan indicated to Humbert Ferrand in the letter of April 16, 1830 (henceforth to be called simply "the Letter"; see pp. 7-9). In the first movement, the title *Rêveries* is applied to the introductory Largo; *Passions*, to the following Allegro. Thus the "double" nature to which the composer refers in the Letter is made clearer than in the printed editions, where *Rêveries—Passions* is combined as a single heading. *Un Bal* and the *Scène aux champs* are now in that order (which evidently

‖‖‖

AVERTISSEMENT

Le Compositeur a eu pour but de développer, dans ce qu'elles ont de musical, différentes situations de la vie d'un artiste. Le plan du drame instrumental, privé du secours de la parole, a besoin d'être exposé d'avance. Le programme[1] suivant doit donc être considéré comme le texte parlé d'un Opéra, servant à amener des morceaux de musique, dont il motive le caractère et l'expression.

1. La distribution de ce programme à l'auditoire, dans les concerts où figure cette symphonie, est indispensable à l'intelligence complète du plan dramatique de l'ouvrage.

became definitive very soon after the Letter was written). The last two movements, the *Marche du supplice* and the *Songe d'une nuit du sabbat*, are paired as parts of the dream: *Première* and *Seconde partie de la vision*. Berlioz for a time vacillated between the title given here to the fourth movement, *Marche du supplice*—"March of Execution" (literally, "Punishment") or "Execution March"—and the one that became standard, *Marche au supplice*—"March to (the Place of) Execution." (There is probably no significance in the eventual change from *du sabbat* to *de sabbat*.)

The story outlined to Ferrand was soon embodied in an official program. A manuscript draft became the source, first of a notice printed in *Figaro* on May 21, 1830, to prepare the public for the projected performance of May 30; next of a version in the *Revue musicale* of November 27, shortly before the actual première; then of the leaflets distributed at the première and at subsequent performances; and finally of the program as printed in the first edition of the score.[5] These documents are all close enough in content and wording to be considered as variations of a single First Program. Here is its definitive form, as published with the score in 1845. (The original old-fashioned spelling has been modernized. The footnotes are those of Berlioz.)

5. A complete transcription of the draft and details of important subsequent changes are given by Julian Tiersot in his immensely helpful "Berlioziana," a serial publication in *Le Ménestrel* (see Bibliography). The fullest description of all variations among the versions of the program is to be found in Nicholas Temperley's edition of the *Fantastic Symphony* for the New Berlioz Edition (see Bibliography), pp. 167–70.

‖‖

NOTE

The composer's intention has been to develop, insofar as they contain musical possibilities, various situations in the life of an artist. The outline of the instrumental drama, which lacks the help of words, needs to be explained in advance. The following program[1] should thus be considered as the spoken text of an opera, serving to introduce the musical movements, whose character and expression it motivates.

1. The distribution of this program to the audience, at concerts where this symphony is to be performed, is indispensable for a complete understanding of the dramatic outline of the work.

PROGRAMME.

PREMIÈRE PARTIE.

RÊVERIES. — PASSIONS.

L'Auteur suppose qu'un jeune musicien, affecté de cette maladie morale qu'un écrivain célèbre appelle le VAGUE DES PASSIONS, voit pour la première fois une femme qui réunit tous les charmes de l'être idéal que rêvait son imagination, et en devient éperdument épris. Par une singulière bizarrerie, l'image chérie ne se présente jamais à l'esprit de l'artiste que liée à une pensée musicale, dans laquelle il trouve un certain caractère passionné, mais noble et timide comme celui qu'il prête à l'objet aimé.

Ce reflet mélodique avec son modèle le poursuivent sans cesse comme une double idée fixe. Telle est la raison de l'apparition constante, dans tous les morceaux de la symphonie, de la mélodie qui commence le premier ALLEGRO. Le passage de cet état de rêverie mélancolique, interrompue par quelques accès de joie sans sujet, à celui d'une passion délirante, avec ses mouvements de fureur, de jalousie, ses retours de tendresse, ses larmes, ses consolations religieuses, est le sujet du premier morceau.

DEUXIÈME PARTIE.

UN BAL.

L'artiste est placé dans les circonstances de la vie les plus diverses, au milieu DU TUMULTE D'UNE FÊTE, dans la paisible contemplation des beautés de la nature; mais partout, à la ville, aux champs, l'image chérie vient se présenter à lui et jeter le trouble dans son âme.

TROISIÈME PARTIE.

SCÈNE AUX CHAMPS.

Se trouvant un soir à la campagne, il entend au loin deux pâtres qui dialoguent un ranz des vaches; ce duo pastoral, le lieu de la scène, le léger bruissement des arbres doucement agités par le vent, quelques motifs d'espérance qu'il a conçus depuis peu, tout concourt à rendre à son coeur un calme inaccoutumé, et à donner à ses idées une couleur plus

PROGRAM

PART ONE
REVERIES—PASSIONS

The author imagines that a young musician, afflicted with that moral disease that a well-known writer calls the *vague des passions*, sees for the first time a woman who embodies all the charms of the ideal being he has imagined in his dreams, and he falls desperately in love with her. Through an odd whim, whenever the beloved image appears before the mind's eye of the artist it is linked with a musical thought whose character, passionate but at the same time noble and shy, he finds similar to the one he attributes to his beloved.

This melodic image and the model it reflects pursue him incessantly like a double *idée fixe*. That is the reason for the constant appearance, in every moment of the symphony, of the melody that begins the first Allegro. The passage from this state of melancholy reverie, interrupted by a few fits of groundless joy, to one of frenzied passion, with its movements of fury, of jealousy, its return of tenderness, its tears, its religious consolations—this is the subject of the first movement.

PART TWO
A BALL

The artist finds himself in the most varied situations—in the midst of *the tumult of a party*, in the peaceful contemplation of the beauties of nature; but everywhere, in town, in the country, the beloved image appears before him and disturbs his peace of mind.

PART THREE
SCENE IN THE COUNTRY

Finding himself one evening in the country, he hears in the distance two shepherds piping a *ranz des vaches* in dialogue. This pastoral duet, the scenery, the quiet rustling of the trees gently brushed by the wind, the hopes he has recently found some reason to entertain—all concur in affording his heart an unaccustomed calm, and in giving a more

riante. Il réfléchit sur son isolement; il espère n'être bientôt plus **seul**. . . . Mais si elle le trompait! . . . Ce mélange d'espoir et de crainte, **ces** idées de bonheur troublées par quelques noirs pressentiments, forment le sujet de l'ADAGIO. A la fin, l'un des pâtres reprend le ranz des vaches; l'autre ne répond plus. . . . Bruit éloigné de tonnerre . . . solitude . . . silence . . .

QUATRIÈME PARTIE.

MARCHE AU SUPPLICE.

Ayant acquis la certitude que son amour est méconnu, l'artiste s'empoisonne avec de l'opium. La dose du narcotique, trop faible **pour** lui donner la mort, le plonge dans un sommeil accompagné des plus horribles visions. Il rêve qu'il a tué celle qu'il aimait, qu'il est condamné, conduit au supplice, et qu'il assiste à SA PROPRE EXÉCUTION. Le cortège s'avance aux sons d'une marche tantôt sombre et farouche, tantôt brillante et solennelle, dans laquelle un bruit sourd de pas graves succède sans transition aux éclats les plus bruyants. A la fin de la marche, les quatre premières mesures de l'IDÉE FIXE reparaissent comme une dernière pensée d'amour interrompue par le coup fatal.

CINQUIÈME PARTIE.

SONGE D'UNE NUIT DU SABBAT.

Il se voit au sabbat, au milieu d'une troupe affreuse d'ombres, de sorciers, de monstres de toute espèce, réunis pour ses funérailles. Bruits étranges, gémissements, éclats de rire, cris lointains auxquels d'autres cris semblent répondre. La mélodie aimée reparait encore, mais elle a perdu son caractère de noblesse et de timidité; ce n'est plus qu'un air de danse ignoble, trivial et grotesque; c'est elle qui vient au sabbat. . . . Rugissement de joie à son arrivée. . . . Elle se mêle à l'orgie diabolique. . . . Glas funèbre, parodie burlesque du DIES IRAE.[1] RONDE DU SABBAT. La ronde du sabbat et le Dies irae ensemble.

1. Hymne chanté dans les ceremonies funèbres de l'Église Catholique.

cheerful color to his ideas. He reflects upon his isolation; he hopes that his loneliness will soon be over.—But what if she were deceiving him!— This mingling of hope and fear, these ideas of happiness disturbed by black presentiments, form the subject of the Adagio. At the end one of the shepherds again takes up the *ranz des vaches*; the other no longer replies.—Distant sound of thunder—loneliness—silence.

PART FOUR
MARCH TO THE SCAFFOLD

Convinced that his love is unappreciated, the artist poisons himself with opium. The dose of the narcotic, too weak to kill him, plunges him into a sleep accompanied by the most horrible visions. He dreams that he has killed his beloved, that he is condemned and led to the scaffold, and that he is witnessing *his own execution*. The procession moves forward to the sounds of a march that is now sombre and fierce, now brilliant and solemn, in which the muffled noise of heavy steps gives way without transition to the noisiest clamor. At the end of the march the first four measures of the *idée fixe* reappear, like a last thought of love interrupted by the fatal blow.

PART FIVE
DREAM OF A WITCHES' SABBATH

He sees himself at the sabbath, in the midst of a frightful troop of ghosts, sorcerers, monsters of every kind, come together for his funeral. Strange noises, groans, bursts of laughter, distant cries which other cries seem to answer. The beloved melody appears again, but it has lost its character of nobility and shyness; it is no more than a dance tune, mean, trivial, and grotesque: it is she, coming to join the sabbath.—A roar of joy at her arrival.—She takes part in the devilish orgy.—Funeral knell, burlesque parody of the *Dies irae*,[1] *sabbath round-dance*. The sabbath round and the *Dies irae* combined.

1. Hymn sung in the funeral rites of the Catholic Church.

A comparison of the texts will show that this program, in diction as well as in content, is not very different from the one outlined in the Letter. Yet there are some important changes, and it is interesting to trace these through the successive stages of the first complete draft (which must have been written soon after the Letter) and the various published versions.

The title of the opening movement is lacking in the draft as well as in the Letter; *Figaro* gives it as *Rêverie.—Existence passionnée*. The final title is more succinct and more neatly balanced; otherwise there seems to be no reason for the alteration. More significant is the change in the nature of the *idée fixe*—or in the composer's conception of it. This is already evident in the draft. There, instead of "grace and nobility," we find the "passionate, but at the same time noble and shy" character familiar from the definitive version. Did this reflect a new attitude toward the theme, toward the heroine of the story, or toward her real-life model? Probably all three, since they are inextricably intertwined.

At the end of the first movement, the "religious consolations" are mentioned only in later, revised versions of the printed leaflet. These reflect a major addition Berlioz made to the closing measures. The seam is clearly visible in the autograph, which discloses that the movement originally ended, much too abruptly, at the present m. 493.

By the time of the draft, the *Ball* had already been placed second, and its description had been established as the one we know. In contradistinction to the account in the Letter, which explains the dance scene specifically, the definitive version refers not only to this movement ("the tumult of a party," "in town") but to the next as well ("the beauties of nature," "in the country"). The final program for the latter, on the other hand, is more elaborate than the original one. In the draft, the implied soliloquy is even quoted in the first person ("I am *alone* in the world ... but I shall soon be no longer *alone*," etc.). Berlioz may have felt later that this melodramatic change of style was too self-revealing, too intense in tone. The ending of this movement, too, must have undergone revision, for the image of the lonely shepherd threatened by the impending storm is found for the first time in the program as printed in the *Revue musicale* just before the première.

The successive descriptions of both the march and the witches' sabbath yield clues to Berlioz's gradually improving state of mind. Whether this was due to the charms of Mlle. Moke, or to the realization that the rumors about Henriette were false, or just to the passing of time, he certainly became less and less hard on his heroine. Compare the mild final version of the hero's reason for taking poison with this one, from the first draft: "Convinced not only that his adored one does not return his love, but that she is incapable of understanding it and moreover has become unworthy of it." (Later versions of this year differ only in detail.) But with respect to the last movement even the draft represents a considerable cooling off from the attitude of the Letter. There, the loved one was described as "a prostitute, fit to take part in such an orgy"; this phrase is never used again. The draft, although somewhat more detailed in its account of the sabbath, is essentially the same as the final version. *Figaro* presents the shortest description of all: it fails to mention the *Dies irae*. No doubt Berlioz felt later that this cut was too drastic and that more explanation here was essential; otherwise the audience might fail to grasp the musical structure of the movement. Hence he restored some of the draft, arriving at the definitive form.

In this cursory examination of the details relating to the individual movements we can thus recognize, in addition to the alterations made for personal reasons, others that reflect revisions of the score, that betray a concern for literary style, and that clarify the musical form. Now we must turn to the crucial introductory remarks; and here it will be necessary to look more closely at the leaflets prepared for the various public performances. Most of these differ only in detail from the one distributed at the première. But two of them, apparently associated with concerts several years later, contain an important addition: a huge footnote, or an essay disguised as a footnote, appended to the introductory paragraph.[6]

Now, the introduction, tentatively formed in the draft, received its definitive wording in the *Figaro* version, from which the leaflets and the first edition do not vary. It is a paragraph obviously intended as an important statement of the composer's esthetic. He tries to explain his approach to symphonic music by invoking the French opéra comique with its alternation of song and spoken dialogue. The opera composer determines which episodes, scenes, and emotional states in his drama are expressible in music; these he sets as musical numbers, connecting them with dialogue ("texte parlé"). In the same way, Berlioz has chosen certain situations from his artist's life that have musical possibilities ("ce qu'elles ont de musical"); these have become the movements of his

6. Temperley, *loc. cit.,* adduces evidence for 1836 and 1838 as the dates of these programs.

symphony. And just as the operatic dialogue leads into the numbers ("amener des morceaux"), explaining their meaning and motivating their expression, so Berlioz's program introduces each movement in turn.

Today all this seems clear enough. Yet Berlioz was evidently prompted to add still further explanation in defense of his point of view against the stubbornness of his critics.[7] Accordingly, in an attempt to make the statement even more emphatic, the revised leaflet gave certain key phrases of the introduction typographical emphasis—*texte parlé d'un opéra, amener, motive le caractère et l'expression,* and especially DANS CE QU'ELLES ONT DE MUSICAL. And the following footnote, which spells out the same message in greater detail, was appended:

> The aim of the program is by no means to copy faithfully what the composer has tried to present in orchestral terms, as some people seem to think; on the contrary, it is precisely in order to fill in the gaps which the use of musical language unavoidably leaves in the development of dramatic thought, that the composer has had to avail himself of written prose to explain and justify the outline of the symphony. He knows very well that music can take the place of neither word nor picture[7]; he has never had the absurd intention of expressing *abstractions* or *moral qualities,* but rather passions and feelings. Nor has he had the even stranger idea of painting *mountains*: he has only wished to reproduce *the melodic style and forms* that characterize the singing of some of the people who live among them, or *the emotion* that the sight of these imposing masses arouses, under certain circumstances, in the soul. If these few lines of program had been of such nature that they could be recited or sung between the movements of the symphony, like the choruses in ancient tragedies, then doubtless this kind of misunderstanding of their meaning would not have arisen. But instead of being heard they must be read; and those who make the curious accusation against which the musician must defend himself fail to realize that if he really entertained the exaggerated and ridiculous opinions about the expressive power of his art that are laid at his door, then by the same token he would have thought this program to be merely a kind of duplication, and hence perfectly useless.

As for the imitation of natural sounds, Beethoven, Gluck, Meyer-

---

7. He had felt misunderstood from the beginning. When the program was printed in the *Revue musicale,* it was preceded by an introductory editorial note that accused Berlioz of trying to use music to paint physical objects and to express abstractions. (Although unsigned, the note can safely be attributed to the editor, François-Joseph Fétis, who produced the journal almost single-handedly. See p. 215.)

beer, Rossini, and Weber have proved, by noteworthy examples, that it has its place in the musical realm. Nevertheless, since the composer of this symphony is convinced that the abuse of such imitation is quite dangerous, that it is of very limited usefulness, and that its happiest effects always verge on caricature, he has never considered this branch of the art as an end, but as a means. And when, for example, in the Scene in the Country, he tries to render the rumbling of distant thunder in the midst of a peaceful atmosphere, it is by no means for the puerile pleasure of imitating this majestic sound, but rather to make *silence* more perceptible, and thus to increase the impression of uneasy sadness and painful isolation that he wants to produce on his audience by the conclusion of this movement.

This, then, is the composer's account of the purpose of the program: not to duplicate the music, but to fill in what the music has left unsaid. And the music was not to reproduce the events of the story, nor to depict its scenery, nor to expound abstract ideas, but to impart the passions and emotions aroused by the dramatic situations. Certainly this defense applies convincingly to the first three movements; less well, it must be confessed, to the last two. But even here it should be noted that the composer's chief concern, in the definitive program of the Finale, is the audience's awareness of what is going on *musically*; they should recognize the clarinet melody as a parody of the *idée fixe*, they should appreciate the polyphonic combination of the *Dies irae* and the round dance. Although we may not completely accept the composer's assurance that the program is never concerned with what he "has tried to present in orchestral terms," and although we may point to passages in which it "describes" the music, we must not assume that the music is thereby reduced to the role of "describing" the program. For the latter may be serving another purpose as well: it may be explicating purely musical relationships. True, Berlioz does not mention this possibility; but, as we have just seen, he certainly takes occasional advantage of it.

One other version of the First Program is worth mentioning, oddly enough because of an astounding bit of misinformation offered on its title page: 1820 is given as the year of the première! It may thus well be the source of a notorious error in Schumann's essay on the symphony.[8] This becomes highly probable if we accept Temperley's conjecture that the pamphlet was printed in 1834 to accompany Liszt's piano transcription, which, as the first publication of the symphony, was the form

---

8. See pp. 223 and 228.

in which Schumann became familiar with it.[9]

The first performance that presented the *Fantastic Symphony* together with its sequel, *Lélio,* took place on the famous occasion of December 9, 1832. Berlioz evidently saw no reason at this time to make any substantial changes in the First Program, which is in fact printed as a preface to the libretto of *Lélio* published by Schlesinger in anticipation of the concert. No doubt the composer had not yet realized that the addition of the monodrama significantly altered the expressive effect of the symphony and that a new program might therefore be desirable. Moreover, he knew very well that combined performances of the two works would be relatively rare. At any rate, the First Program remained standard for many years. It was, as we know, the one included in the published score of 1845. Indeed, this edition made no mention of *Lélio,* either on the title page or in the program, presumably because the mono-

9. Temperley, *loc. cit.*

Avertissement.

Le programme suivant doit être distribué à l'auditoire toutes les fois que la symphonie fantastique est exécutée *dramatiquement* et suivie, en conséquence, du monodrame de Lélio,[1] qui termine et complète *l'épisode de la vie d'un artiste.* En pareil cas, l'orchestre invisible est disposé sur la scène d'un théâtre derrière la toile baissée.[2]

Si on exécute la symphonie isolément dans un concert, cette disposition n'est plus nécessaire; on peut même à la rigueur se dispenser de distribuer le programme, en conservant seulement le titre des cinq morceaux; la symphonie (l'auteur l'espère) pouvant offrir en soi un intérêt musical indépendant de toute intention dramatique.

PROGRAMME
de la Symphonie.

Un jeune musicien d'une sensibilité maladive et d'une imagination ardente, s'empoisonne avec de l'opium dans un accès de désespoir amoureux. La dose de narcotique, trop faible pour lui donner la mort,

1. Publié chez Richault à Paris.
2. Voyez pour les détails de cette mise en scène la préface de la grande partition de Lélio.

drama was still unready for publication. Hence Berlioz must have assumed that the symphony would normally be performed alone.

At some point, however, a new program was devised, specifically designed for performances that included *Lélio.* That work was published in 1855, and it is likely that the Second Program replaced the First in the printed scores with this eventuality—or actuality—in view. The version reproduced below, taken from the edition of Brandus & Dufour described on p. 19, refers in footnotes to the availability of the score of *Lélio.*

The new program was accompanied in parallel columns by a German translation that indicated the spread of Berlioz's international reputation. He had introduced the symphony to Germany in 1842 and obviously hoped for further performances there.

Here, then, is the Second Program. As before, the original orthography has been modernized, and a few misprints have been corrected.

Note

The following program should be distributed to the audience whenever the Fantastic Symphony is executed *dramatically* and consequently followed by the monodrama *Lélio,*[1] which finishes and completes the *Episode from the Life of an Artist.* In such cases, the orchestra should be unseen, placed on the stage of a theater behind the lowered curtain.[2]

If the symphony alone is performed in a concert, this arrangement is no longer essential; if necessary, one can even dispense with distributing the program, keeping only the titles of the five movements. The symphony by itself (the author hopes) can afford musical interest independent of any dramatic purpose.

PROGRAM
of the Symphony

A young musician of morbidly sensitive temperament and fiery imagination poisons himself with opium in a fit of lovesick despair. The dose of the narcotic, too weak to kill him, plunges him into a deep slumber

1. Published by Richault, Paris.
2. For the details of this mise-en-scène see the preface to the full score of *Lélio.*

le plonge dans un lourd sommeil accompagné des plus étranges visions, pendant lequel ses sensations, ses sentiments, ses souvenirs se traduisent dans son cerveau malade, en pensées et en images musicales. La femme aimée, elle-même, est devenue pour lui une mélodie et comme une idée fixe qu'il retrouve et qu'il entend partout.

1er PARTIE.

RÊVERIES, PASSIONS.

Il se rappelle d'abord ce malaise de l'âme, *ce vague des passions*, ces mélancolies, ces joies sans sujet qu'il éprouva avant d'avoir vu celle qu'il aime; puis l'amour volcanique qu'elle lui inspira subitement, ses délirantes angoisses, ses jalouses fureurs, ses retours de tendresse, ses consolations religieuses.

2me PARTIE.

UN BAL.

Il retrouve l'aimée dans un bal au milieu du tumulte d'une fête brillante.

3me PARTIE.

SCÈNE AUX CHAMPS.

Un soir d'été a la campagne, il entend deux pâtres qui dialoguent un Ranz des vaches; ce duo pastoral, le lieu de la scène, le léger bruissement des arbres doucement agités par le vent, quelques motifs d'espoir qu'il a conçus depuis peu, tout concourt à rendre à son coeur un calme inaccoutumé, à donner à ses idées une couleur plus riante; mais *elle* apparait de nouveau, son coeur se serre, de douloureux pressentiments l'agitent, si elle le trompait. . . . . L'un des pâtres reprend sa naïve mélodie, l'autre ne répond plus. Le soleil se couche . . . bruit éloigné du tonnerre . . . . . . solitude . . . . . silence . . . . .

4me PARTIE.

MARCHE AU SUPPLICE.

Il rève qu'il a tué celle qu'il aimait, qu'il est condamné à mort, conduit au supplice. Le cortége s'avance, aux sons d'une marche tantôt sombre et farouche, tantôt brillante et solennelle, dans laquelle un bruit

accompanied by the strangest visions, during which his sensations, his emotions, his memories are transformed in his sick mind into musical thoughts and images. The loved one herself has become a melody to him, an *idée fixe* as it were, that he encounters and hears everywhere.

PART I

REVERIES, PASSIONS

He recalls first that soul-sickness, that *vague des passions*, those depressions, those groundless joys, that he experienced before he first saw his loved one; then the volcanic love that she suddenly inspired in him, his frenzied suffering, his jealous rages, his returns to tenderness, his religious consolations.

PART II

A BALL

He encounters the loved one at a dance in the midst of the tumult of a brilliant party.

PART III

SCENE IN THE COUNTRY

One summer evening in the country, he hears two shepherds piping a *ranz des vaches* in dialogue; this pastoral duet, the scenery, the quiet rustling of the trees gently brushed by the wind, the hopes he has recently found some reason to entertain—all concur in affording his heart an unaccustomed calm, and in giving a more cheerful color to his ideas. But she appears again, he feels a tightening in his heart, painful presentiments disturb him—what if she were deceiving him?—One of the shepherds takes up his simple tune again, the other no longer answers. The sun sets—distant sound of thunder—loneliness—silence.

PART IV

MARCH TO THE SCAFFOLD

He dreams that he has killed his beloved, that he is condemned to death and led to the scaffold. The procession moves forward to the sounds of a march that is now somber and fierce, now brilliant and solemn, in

sourd de pas graves succède sans transition aux éclats les plus bruyants. A la fin, *l'idée fixe* reparait un instant comme une dernière pensée d'amour interrompue par le coup fatal.

5me PARTIE.

SONGE D'UNE NUIT DU SABBAT.

Il se voit au sabbat, au milieu d'une troupe affreuse d'ombres, de sorciers, de monstres, de toute espèce réunis pour ses funérailles. Bruits étranges, gémissements, éclats de rire, cris lointains auxquels d'autres cris semblent répondre. *La mélodie-aimée* reparait encore; mais elle a perdu son caractère de noblesse et de timidité; ce n'est plus qu'un air de danse ignoble, trivial et grotesque; c'est *elle* qui vient au sabbat. . . . Rugissement de joie à son arrivée. . . . Elle se mèle à l'orgie diabolique. . . . Glas funèbre, parodie burlesque du *Dies irae*. Ronde du sabbat. La ronde du sabbat et le *Dies irae* ensemble.

Two questions immediately demand discussion. Why did Berlioz extend the opium dream so as to include all five movements? Why did he suggest performance without the distribution of the program?

The answers can only be conjectured. With regard to the first, the connection with *Lélio* may well have been the determining factor. *Lélio* depicted the awakening; it was an extended work with six movements interspersed by long monologues. It might then make for better dramatic balance to allow the entire symphony to represent the dream. Such a plan would also be more immediately apprehensible to the audience: symphony = dream, monodrama = awakening.

As for the permission to dispense with the program altogether, I think one should take at face value the composer's hope that the work would offer sufficient "musical interest independent of any dramatic purpose." In this wish he was probably encouraged by the artistic success of *Harold in Italy*, a program symphony, to be sure, but one without a program. There he had found the titles alone sufficed. And after all, the extension of the dream through the entire symphony implied, in a way, a denigration of the whole programmatic idea. Berlioz certainly realized that whatever music can or cannot portray, there is no way that music alone can distinguish between the depiction (a) of an experience, (b) of which the muffled sound of heavy steps gives way without transition to the noisiest clamor. At the end, the *idée fixe* returns for a moment, like a last thought of love interrupted by the fatal blow.

PART V

DREAM OF A WITCHES' SABBATH

[The program for this movement reproduces the First Program.]

a memory of the experience, and (c) of a dream about the experience. The distinction between waking and dream in the earlier program had thus been artificial and nonmusical, and the obliteration of the division might have been a confession that the descriptive powers of music were even more limited than the composer had hitherto admitted. It is possible, then, that the new program was his way of telling the audience: "Look, don't take all this too seriously; it's only a dream. The main thing is the music."

HECTOR BERLIOZ

On Imitation in Music †

Berlioz's essay *De l'Imitation musicale* is his most complete and explicit statement of the aims and limitations of program music. It appeared in the issues of January 1 and 8, 1837, of the *Revue et Gazette musicale de Paris*, of which Berlioz was at that time the editor.

Giuseppe Carpani (1752–1825), whose essay furnished Berlioz with a point of attack for his own, was an Italian librettist and writer on musical subjects. The book in question is *Le Haydine, ovvero lettere su la vita e le opere del celebre Giuseppe Haydn* (1812).

The translation is by Jacques Barzun, with the exception of a few passages omitted by him, which I have restored. These are all indicated by brackets.

I

Let us begin by discussing *imitation* in music, not in the technical sense which refers to fugue and the fugal style, but in the sense of producing certain noises which describe or depict by musical means objects whose existence we are aware of only through our eyes. This notable element of art, which not a single great composer of any school has neglected to use, whether or not his attempts were successful, and which admittedly has seduced more than one into ridiculous and deplorable errors, has seldom been treated with any fullness or examined with judgment. [The subject is one of great importance nevertheless; from time to time sentinels at the outposts of musical journalism put the question as a challenge, but there is never any response.] I shall therefore try to throw some light on the darker side of its theory, while seeking the criterion by which to determine when its application ceases to be art and falls into absurdity after exhibiting the silly and the grotesque.

† From *Pleasures of Music*, ed. by Jacques Barzun, New York, 1951. Reprinted by permission of Mr. Barzun and The Viking Press, Inc. The essay is there entitled "The Limits of Music," and is translated by Mr. Barzun.

M. Joseph Carpani, the excellent Italian critic to whom we owe, among other things, a volume of letters on the life and works of Haydn, will help us in our search. His views on the matter seem those of a man gifted with musical good sense and a proper feeling about the true limits of the art of music. Yet he appears to me not to have sufficiently brought out the main features of the subject. Hence the present attempt to fill in the gaps left by his discussion, which I mean to follow step by step.

In one of his letters about the famous oratorio *The Creation*, in which Haydn makes frequent use of the descriptive style, M. Carpani remarks that long before Haydn composers had been making use of the imitative means open to the musician; of these the critic distinguishes two kinds—the physical and the emotional. The first he calls direct, the second indirect.

> By direct imitation (says M. Carpani), I mean the imitation of sounds as they occur in the throats of animals, or as they are made by the air vibrating in different ways around solid bodies. [This element turns all bodies into musical instruments, provided that they offer some resistance.] The air soughs through foliage, bellows in caverns, murmurs along uneven places, etc., all of which it is proper for music to imitate, even though it be not its highest prerogative. Such imitations are difficult and deserve credit. It is said that a Greek was once asked to go and hear a man whistle like a nightingale. "Not I," replied the Greek, "I have heard the actual bird." The reply has been wrongly lauded. "My dear logician," I should have said to him, "it is precisely because the song is not made by a bird that it is worth hearing and admiring. If some one told you to look at a battle painted by Giulio Romano and you replied, 'I have seen a real battle,' what sense would there be in the rejoinder? It is exactly because you have witnessed real battles that you must find pleasure in seeing art reproduce the likeness with a little colored earth."

Here M. Carpani seems to me to go seriously astray by borrowing an argument from a comparison with painting. That art may not indeed have any other object than to reproduce with fidelity, to give a beautiful imitation of Nature; whereas music is in most cases an art *sui generis*. It is sufficient unto itself, and possesses the power to charm without having recourse to any kind of imitation. Painting, moreover, cannot encroach on the domain of music; but music can by its own means act upon the imagination in such a way as to engender sensations analogous to those produced by graphic art. This point, however, belongs to the second part of our subject, that which M. Carpani calls indirect or emotional imitation. As to the first, the direct or physical imitation of the sounds and noises of Nature, here is what I would say about it and what our author fails to bring out:

If we are to accept imitation among musical devices without detract-ing from music's independent power or nobleness, the first condition is that imitation shall virtually never be an *end* but only a *means*; that it shall never be considered (except very rarely) the main musical idea, but only the complement of that idea, joined to the main idea in a logical and natural manner.

The second condition to making imitation acceptable is that it shall concern something worthy of holding the listener's attention, and that it shall not (at least in serious works) be used to render sounds, motions, or objects that belong outside the sphere which art cannot desert without self-degradation.

The third condition is that the imitation, without aping reality as by an exact substitution of Nature for art, shall nonetheless be close enough for the composer's intent to avoid misconception in the minds of an attentive audience.

The fourth and last condition is that this physical imitation shall never occur in the very spot where *emotional* imitation (expressiveness) is called for, and thus encroach with descriptive futilities when the drama is proceeding apace and passion alone deserves a voice.

To illustrate and support the foregoing distinctions, I shall take examples from the great masters of music and poetry (for in this matter music and poetry have a common stake), and I shall begin with Bee-thoven. It might seem as if the "Storm" in the Pastoral Symphony were a magnificent exception to our first rule, which allows imitation only as a means and not as an end. For this symphonic movement is wholly given over to the reproduction of the divers noises heard during a violent storm which breaks suddenly over some village festivities. First a few drops of rain, then the rising wind, the thunder grumbling dully in the distance, the birds seeking shelter; finally the approaching gale, the boughs that split, men and animals scattering with cries of dismay, the shattering bolts of lightning, the floodgates of heaven opening, the ele-ments let loose—chaos.

And yet this sublime depiction, which outstrips anything that had ever been attempted in the genre, actually falls within the category of *contrasts* and *dramatic effects*, which are required by the scope of the work. For it is preceded and followed by gentle and smiling scenes to which it acts as a foil. That this is so may be tested by imagining this storm transplanted into another composition in which its presence would not be motivated: it would unquestionably lose a great deal of its effectiveness. Hence this piece of imitation is strictly speaking a means of achieving contrast, devised and managed with the incalculable power of genius.

In *Fidelio*, on the other hand, a work by the same composer, we find another piece of musical imitation of very different purport from the one just reviewed. It occurs in the famous duet at the grave: the jailer and Fidelio dig the place where Florestan is to be buried. Half-way through their toil the pair unearth a large rock and roll it with difficulty to one side. At that point the double basses of the orchestra play a strange and very brief figure—not to be confused with the ostinato phrase of the basses which runs through the whole piece—by which it is said Beethoven wished to imitate *the dull sound of the rolling stone.*

Now this imitation, being in no way necessary either to the drama or to the effectiveness of the music, is really an end in itself for the composer: he imitates in order to imitate—and at once he falls into error, for there is in such imitation no poetry, no drama, no truth. It is a sad piece of childishness, which one is equally grieved and surprised to have to complain of in a great master. The same could be said of Handel, if it be true—as is commonly said—that in his oratorio *Israel in Egypt* he tried to reproduce the flight of locusts, and this to the point of shaping accordingly the rhythmic figure of the vocal parts. Surely that is a regrettable imitation of a subject even more regrettable—unworthy of music in general and of the noble and elevated style of the oratorio.

Haydn, on the contrary, in his essentially descriptive works *The Creation* and *The Seasons*, does not seem to have lowered his style appreciably when, in order to follow the poem, he applied imitation to such agreeable noises as the warbling of turtledoves—an imitation that is, moreover, quite exact.

This brings us back to Beethoven and the Pastoral. There has been frequent criticism of the song of the three birds toward the end of the "Scene by the Brook." As regards the suitability of this imitation, it seems obvious enough. Most of the quiet voices of the waters, earth, and sky naturally find a place here and contribute easily to the serene magnificence of the landscape, but they are not all equally capable of faithful rendering. Beethoven wanted to make the quail, the cuckoo, and the nightingale heard in his orchestra. Now, the first two are unmistakable from the very outset, whereas it is clear that no listener would ever recognize the nightingale in its pretended imitation without being told. The reason is that the fixed sounds of the quail and cuckoo are available in our scale and our instruments, but the voice of the nightingale, sometimes plaintive, sometimes brilliant, and ever irregular, is not imitable. It is odd that this fact of observation has escaped the many composers who have similarly tried and failed to ape the elusive vocalizations of the warbler of dusk.

[On the other hand, several composers have brought ridicule upon themselves by using certain sounds, in all their antimusical reality, as substitutes for themselves. Thus an Italian composer, whose name escapes me, wrote a symphony on the death of Werther[1]; he felt that the best way to imitate the pistol shot of the suicide was to shoot a real pistol in the orchestra. This is the height of absurdity. When Méhul and Weber needed the sound of firearms, the former for the overture to *Le jeune Henri*,[2] the latter for the Infernal Hunt in *Der Freischütz*, they succeeded admirably, without overstepping the bounds of art, by using a simple kettledrum stroke, deftly introduced. If M. Meyerbeer, in *Les Huguenots*, used real bells instead of an imperfect orchestral imitation, that is because such a solution was dictated by the dramatic situation. The terrifying effect of that ill-omened clangor vibrating throughout the opera house proves that he was right; besides, even if success were not the best of all justifications, one could still quite properly point out that bells are musical instruments after all, and that no happier chance of using them has ever arisen.][3]

One may mention other imitations which reason does not exactly reprove but which have been so long in the public domain that they have become vulgar; so that the musician who uses them must show rare tact or strong inspiration to ennoble them or give them the appearance of freshness. In one of the duets of *William Tell*, for example, under Arnold's words "I seek the field of glory," there is a prolonged rhythmic pedal point for trumpets. Its effect seems to me commonplace, or at any rate open to criticism of a kind that a man of judgment such as M. Rossini should not make himself liable to. On the other hand, in Gluck's *Armide* the clamor of war with which the composer accompanies Dunois' exclamation "Our general summons you!" makes the most phlegmatic listener thrill with enthusiasm; it will remain, regardless of the revolutions of taste, as one of the most dazzling strokes of genius.

When, finally, physical imitation is used as a means, there is a pitfall

1. I have been unable to track this reference down. It is certainly true that *Werther* inspired a great deal of music, well before Massenet. [*Editor*]
2. An opera (1797) by Étienne-Nicolas Méhul (1763–1817). [*Editor*]
3. Except, perhaps, in the last movement of the *Fantastic Symphony*. [*Editor*]

into which some of the greatest poets have fallen, and to which I shall draw the attention of musicians. [This is the difficulty of confining it to appropriate situations, of taking particular care never to substitute it for the most powerful of all forms of imitation—the one that reproduces the emotions and the passions: *expressiveness*.] When Talma, playing Orestes, used to hiss the *s*'s as he exclaimed, *"Pour qui sont ces serpents qui sifflent sur vos têtes?"*[4] far from being terrifying he always made me want to laugh. For it seemed to me clear, then as now, that this solicitude of Orestes to imitate the hissing of serpents when his soul is filled with terror, his heart with despair, and his head with ghostly visions, was directly opposed to any idea we may form of what is dramatically natural and likely. Obviously Orestes is not *describing* the Furies; he imagines that he is actually seeing them. He hails them, pleads with them, defies them; and one must be a very docile spectator not to find comic a piece of imitation ascribed to such a sufferer at such a juncture.

As against this, Virgil's many imitative passages strike me as most felicitous, for he has taken care to put them in the narratives made by his characters or in the descriptions for which the poet himself is responsible, e.g.,

> *Ruit alto a culmine Troia.*
> *Nox atra cava circumvolat umbra.*
> *Quadrupedante putrem sonitu quatit ungula campum.*
> [*Procumbit humi bos.*][5]

[These are admirable imitations. But suppose that the next to last, instead of forming part of an *epic recital*, had been given by the poet as a *dramatic exclamation* to a wounded knight, hanging with one foot in the stirrup, dragged by his horse through the midst of the battle: let us agree that the coolness of this man, engaged in describing the gallop of the horses that are trampling him, would have seemed to us completely ridiculous. Is Orestes much less so?

In the second section of this essay we shall examine the second type of imitation, which M. Carpani calls *indirect* or *emotional*, and which we shall call, according to the specific case, *musical metaphor* or *expression*.]

---

4. "For whom are those snakes that hiss around your heads?," from Racine's *Andromaque*, V, 5. François Joseph Talma (1763–1826) was considered the greatest French tragedian of his day. [*Editor*]

5. All from the *Aeneid*:
"Troy topples from its lofty summit." (II, 290)
"Black night envelops us in the hollow shadow of her wings." (II, 360)
"The sound of galloping hoofs shakes the soft earth." (VIII, 596)
"The ox falls to the ground." (V, 481) [*Editor*]

II

[The aim of the second kind of imitation, as we have said before, is to reproduce the intonations of the passions and the emotions, and even to trace a musical image, or metaphor, of objects that can only be *seen*. But before we turn to it, let me say a few words more on physical imitation. This imitation, according to M. Carpani, was carried to such an extreme in seventeenth-century Italy that the composer Melani, in his opera *Il Potestà di Colognole*,[6] set the following words to music, and tried to make the instruments play the roles of the animals mentioned:

> *Talor la granochiella nel pantano*
> *Per allegrezza canta: qua qua rà;*
> *Tribbia il grillo: tri, tri, tri:*
> *L'agnellino fa: bè bè;*
> *L'usignuolo: chiù chiù chiù;*
> *Ed il gal: curi chi chi.*

> Sometimes the frog in the swamp
> Sings for joy: brekekekex;
> The cricket threshes: cri, cri, cri;
> And the little lamb goes: baa, baa;
> The nightingale: jug, jug, jug;
> And the rooster: cockadoodledoo.

But well before Melani, in ancient times, the Greeks used this kind of realistic imitation in their plays: witness Aristophanes's comedies *The Frogs* and *The Birds*. Although Haydn used it in his famous oratorios only in moderation and with discretion, sometimes one cannot help regretting that the subjects at his disposal often led him, too, into similar puerilities. Doubtless he appreciated them at their true value; and perhaps he made a place for them in his scores only to please a few members of the society in which he moved—music fanciers who were much more interested in these instrumental tours de force than in his most splendid inspirations. Baron van Swieten,[7] among others, kept annoying the composer by insisting that he should put the sound of frogs into *The Seasons*. Haydn held firm and refused to mire himself in the marsh in imitation of the Greek poet just to conform to the taste of the hyperclassical van Swieten.

6. Jacopo Melani (1623–76). The opera appeared in 1656. [*Editor*]

7. Gottfried, Freiherr van Swieten (1730–1803), director of the Imperial Library in Vienna and a well-known amateur musician. He translated the English texts of *The Creation* and *The Seasons* into German. [*Editor*]

The best physical imitation is one which, without falling into either of the two opposite excesses mentioned in Part I, would be faithful enough to prevent its subject from being mistaken, yet would not reproduce its sound exactly as it is in nature; on the contrary, such imitation would merely trace the outline of its subject, and touch it with delicate color. That is enough for physical imitation.]

The kind of imitation that M. Carpani calls *emotional* is designed to arouse in us by means of sound the notion of the several passions of the heart, and to awaken solely through the sense of hearing the impressions that human beings experience only through the other senses. Such is the goal of *expression, depiction,* or *musical metaphors.* As regards expressive power, I doubt whether the arts of drawing and even of poetry can equal music. It is only the infatuation of a certain celebrated composer's followers, joined to their total lack of musical feeling and education, that has enabled them to defend their idol on the ground that all musical accents were interchangeable, whence it followed that the composer of *Otello*[8] was not guilty of nonsense or absurdity, since no music could be *true.* He himself refuted them in masterly fashion by his score of *William Tell.* But it would be tedious to dwell on the point.

Musical *depiction,* as I shall show in a moment, is not quite the same thing as a musical *metaphor* and does not seem to me to be nearly so genuine a possibility. The famous naturalist Lacépède,[9] who among his scientific colleagues passed for a very fine composer, says somewhere that "since music has only sounds at its disposal, it can act only through sound. Hence in order to produce the signs of our perceptions these signs must themselves be sounds." But how can one express musically things that make no sound whatever, such as the denseness of a forest, the coolness of a meadow, the progress of the moon? Lacépède answers, "By retracing the feelings these things inspire in us." And our Italian critic finds this sort of imitation worthy, admirable, enchanting. He deems it the musical sublime. I am far from sharing that opinion, and I incline rather to think him mistaken—deceived, like many other writers, by a play on words or if you prefer, by the lack of precision noticeable in the terms that define the subject.

Is there, for example, any single fixed manner in which we are

8. Obviously, Rossini's *Otello* (1816) is the one meant here. [*Editor*]
9. Bernard Germaine Étienne de La Ville, Comte de Lacépède (1756–1825), French naturalist who was also an amateur composer. His *Poétique de la musique,* an essay in two volumes, appeared 1781–85. [*Editor*]

affected by the sight of a forest, a meadow, or the moon in the sky?
Assuredly not. The woods whose shade and coolness will draw a reminiscent sigh from the happy lover will make the jealous or jilted man gnash
his teeth, and will fill his heart with gall at the thought of his happy
rival. Meanwhile the hunter will approach it full of eagerness and expansive joy, whereas the maiden will look upon it with secret fears. Now
music will easily express blissful love, jealousy, carefree gaiety, anxious
modesty, violent threats, suffering and fear, but whether these feelings
have been caused by the sight of a forest or anything else, music is forever incapable of telling us. And the pretension to extend the prerogatives of musical expression beyond these already spacious limits strikes
me as wholly untenable. Hence there are hardly any composers of real
merit who have wasted their time in pursuit of such an illusion. Their
business was quite other, and their achievement far superior to these
so-called imitations. If some few have occasionally given up music in
favor of something which, after all, is neither music nor painting—and
thus given up substance for shadow, [like the dog in the fable]—I am
inclined to think that art as a whole has not lost much thereby, and that
in their case substance and shadow equally lacked merit.

Handel, it is true, tried in one of his works to depict a natural phenomenon which has nothing to do with sound or even with silent
rhythm, and which affects no one, I should imagine, in any determinate
manner—the phenomenon of falling snow. I find it quite impossible to
understand how he hoped to get a grip on such a subject once he had
made up his mind to imitate it in music.[10]

I shall be told, perhaps, that there exist admirable examples of musical depiction which must be taken account of, if only as exceptions. But
on looking closer it becomes clear that these poetical beauties in no way
overstep the vast circle, within which our art is circumscribed by its very
nature. For these imitations are not in fact offered us as pictures of
objects but only as images or analogues. They help to reawaken comparable sensations by means which music undoubtedly possesses. Yet even so,
before the original of these images can be recognized, it is strictly
required that the hearer be notified of the composer's intent by some
indirect means, and that the point of the comparison be patent. Thus
Rossini is thought to have depicted in *William Tell* the movement of

10. Paul Henry Lang suggests that Berlioz may have mistakenly recalled the chorus
from *Israel in Egypt* depicting hailstones, but I suspect that he was thinking of a passage
in Haydn's *Creation*. [*Editor*]

men rowing. In point of fact all he has done is to mark in the orchestra a *rinforzando* accented at regular intervals—an *image* of the rhythmic straining of the oarsmen, whose arrival has been announced by the other characters.

Again, Weber is credited with having painted the moonlight in the accompaniment to Agatha's aria in the second act of *Der Freischütz*; this is because the calm, veiled, and melancholy coloring of the harmonies and the chiaroscuro of the instrumental timbre form a faithful metaphor or *image* of the pale light of the moon, and, moreover, admirably express the dreaminess of lovers beneath the moon, whose assistance Agatha just then invokes.

Of certain other compositions one may say that they represent a broad expanse or infinity itself, because the composer has been able to suggest to the ear, through the breadth of his melodies, the grandeur and clarity of the harmony and the majesty of the rhythm—all of these being set off by contrary effects—impressions analogous to those a climber might feel on the summit of a mountain when beholding in space the splendid panorama suddenly unrolled *before his eyes*. And here, too, the truth of the *image* will appear only if the listener has taken the pains to inform himself ahead of time about the subject treated by the musician.

It is evident that the possibility of *arousing emotions by images,* that only words sung or spoken can identify, is very far from sustaining the ambitious and vain design of positively denoting by musical means objects that are inaudible or rhythmless.

There is to be sure another kind of *image* that fastens on the words of vocal music, but it succeeds only in shackling expression at large by dwelling on accessory details regardless of meaning. This sort of image is almost invariably childish or petty. [Spontini, it is true, found a sublime example in these verses of *La Vestale*:

> *Les dieux, pour signaler leur colère éclatante,*
> *Vont-ils dans le chaos replonger l'univers?*[11]

But for this magnificent fall from the first to the second syllable of the word *chaos,*] how many asininities of this sort could be pointed out in the works of more or less renowned composers! Some cannot come to the word "Heaven" without leaping to a high note: another would think it a disgrace not to speak of Hell in the lowest vocal register. One makes the

---

11. "Will the gods, in an outburst of wrath, plunge the universe again into chaos?," from Act II of *La Vestale* (1807) by Gasparo Spontini (1774–1851). *[Editor]*

dawn rise and another makes the night fall. Nothing is so unbearable as this mania for continually playing on words—a mania which, it must be said, is gradually being cured. For to judge from J. J. Rousseau's assault upon his contemporaries, it was never more prevalent nor more acute than among the French musicians of the last century.[12]

12. It is true that Rousseau violently attacked French composers in his *Lettre sur la musique française* (1753) and elsewhere, but his grounds were not those ascribed to him here. By inference one could assume his opposition to such practices; see Chapter XIV of his *Essai sur l'origine des langues* (1753). [*Editor*]

THE SCORE
OF THE SYMPHONY

INSTRUMENTATION

2 Flutes (*Fl.*)
 II doubles on Piccolo (*Fl. picc.*)
2 Oboes (*Ob.*)
 II doubles on English horn (*C. ingl.*)
2 Clarinets (*Clar.*) in B♭ (*B*), A, C, E♭ (*Es*)
4 Bassoons (*Fag.*)

4 Horns (*Cor.*) in E♭ (*Es*), E, F, B♭ (*B*), C
2 Cornets (*Ctti.*) in B♭ (*B*), A, G
2 Trumpets (*Tr.*) in C, B♭ (*B*), E♭ (*Es*)
3 Trombones (*Tromb.*)
2 Ophicleides (*Oph.*)

Timpani (*Timp.*)
Bass drum (*Gr. Tamb.*)
Snare drum (*Tamburo*)
Cymbals (*Cinelli*)
Bells (*Campane*)
2 Harps (*Arpa*)

Violin I (*Viol. I*)
Violin II (*Viol. II*)
Viola
Cello (*Vcello., Vcllo.*)
Double Bass (*C. B.*)

I

Dreams– Passions   Rêveries, Passions

49

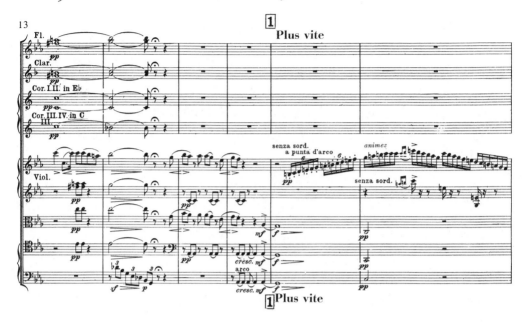

Allegro agitato e appassionato assai (♩ = 132)

Une mesure de ce mouvement équivaut au quart de la précédente.
One bar of this tempo is equal to a quarter-bar of the preceding.

Allegro agitato e appassionato assai. (♩ = 132.)

463 **Tempo I più animato**

474 **Tempo I più animato**

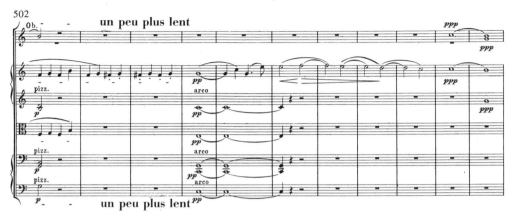

Religiosamente

513
Tout l'orchestre aussi doux que possible
The whole orchestra as soft as possible

Religiosamente

II

A Ball   Un bal

302

318

rallent.--- **Tempo I con fuoco**

rallent.--- **Tempo I con fuoco**

358

III

In the Country   Scène aux champs

103
42 animez un peu
Fl.
Ob.
Clar.
Cor. I.II in F.
Cor. III in Es.
Cor. IV in C.
Fag.
Timp. I.
Baguettes de bois
Wooden drum-sticks
cresc.
a 2.
unis.
Viol.
42 animez un peu
109
rallent.
Tempo I
dim.
p morendo
pp
Cor. I.II.
Cor. III.
Cor. IV.
tr.
pizz.
Soli
rallent.
Tempo I

IV

March to the Scaffold   Marche au supplice

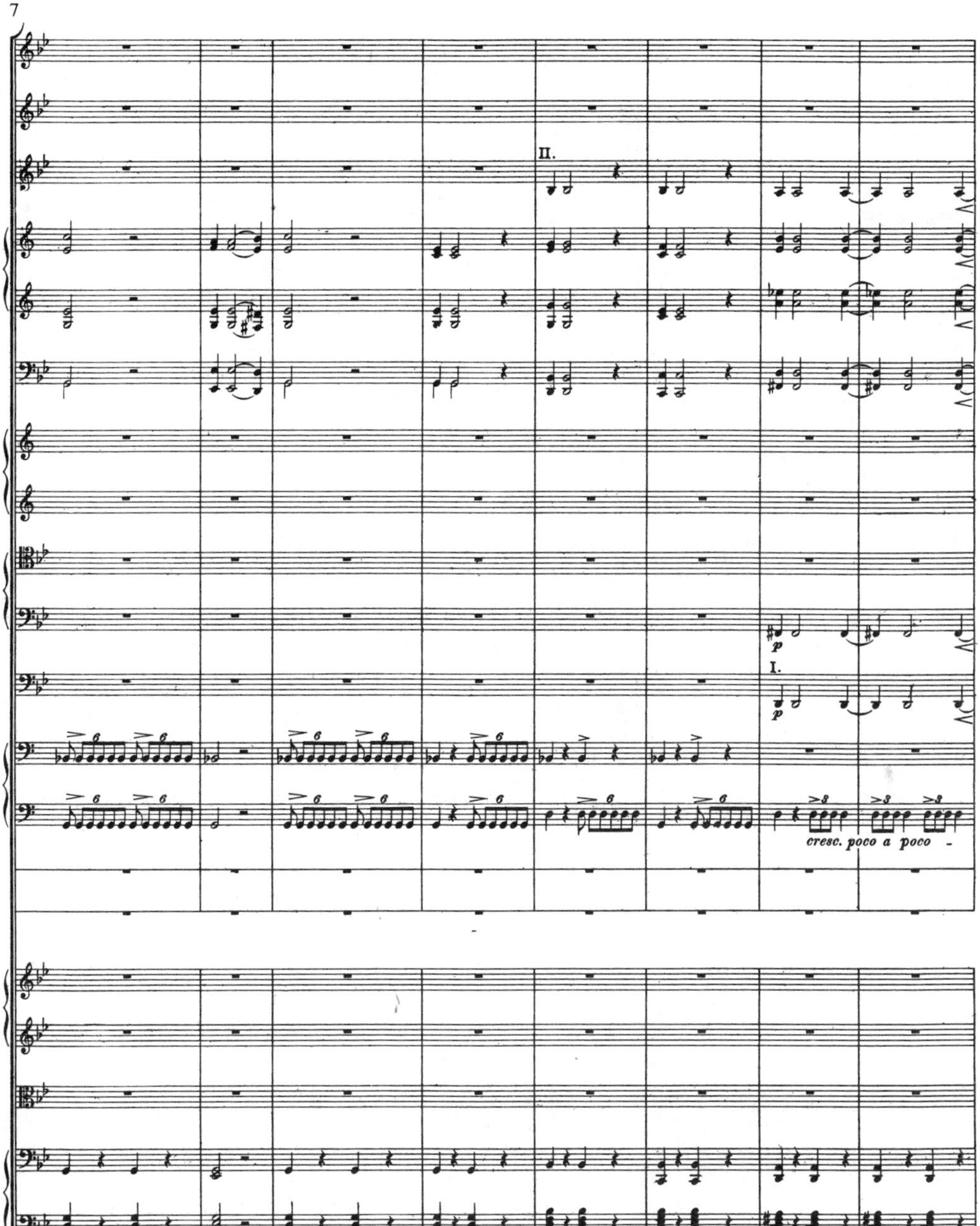
7
II.
I.
p
p
cresc. poco a poco -

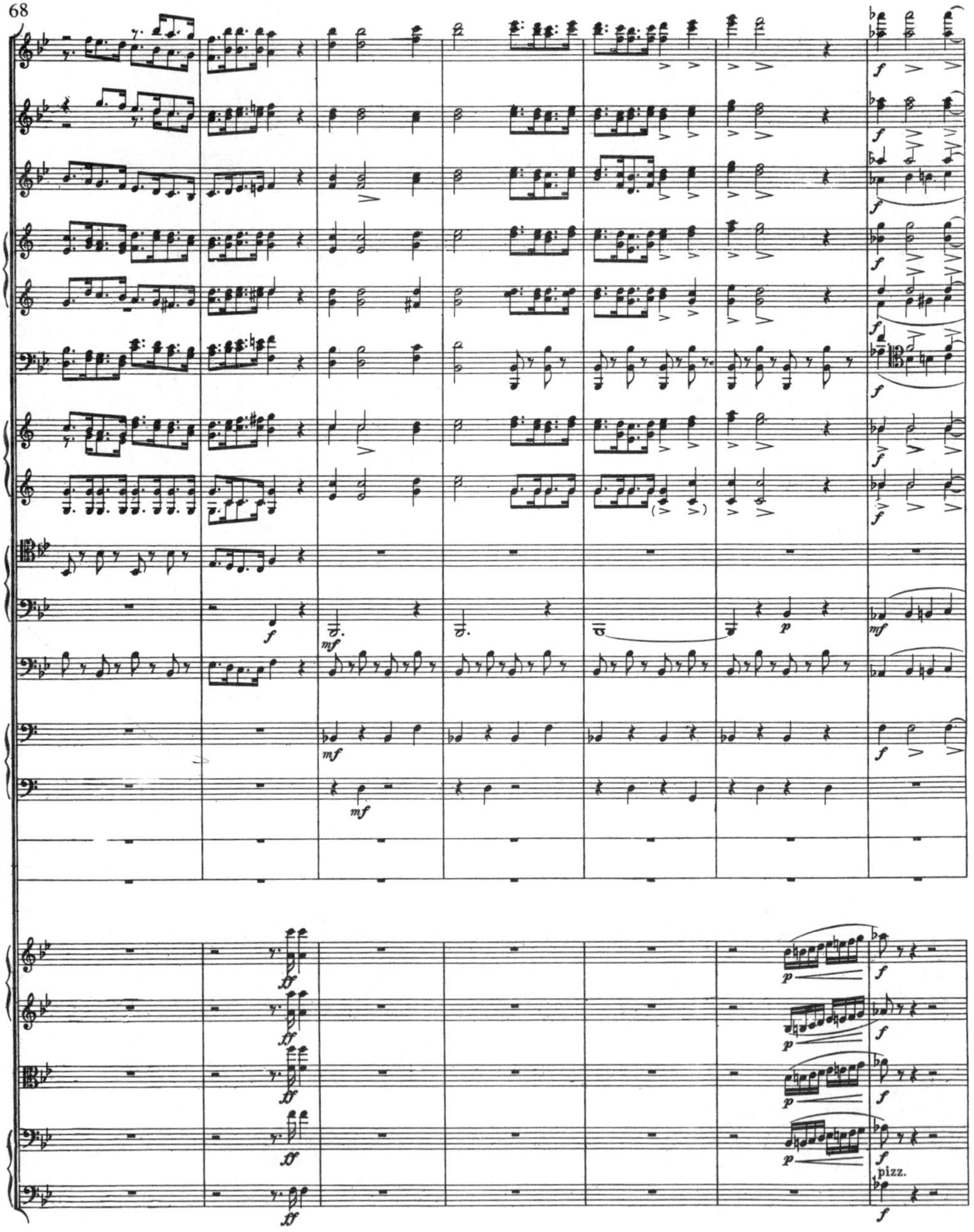
68
pizz.

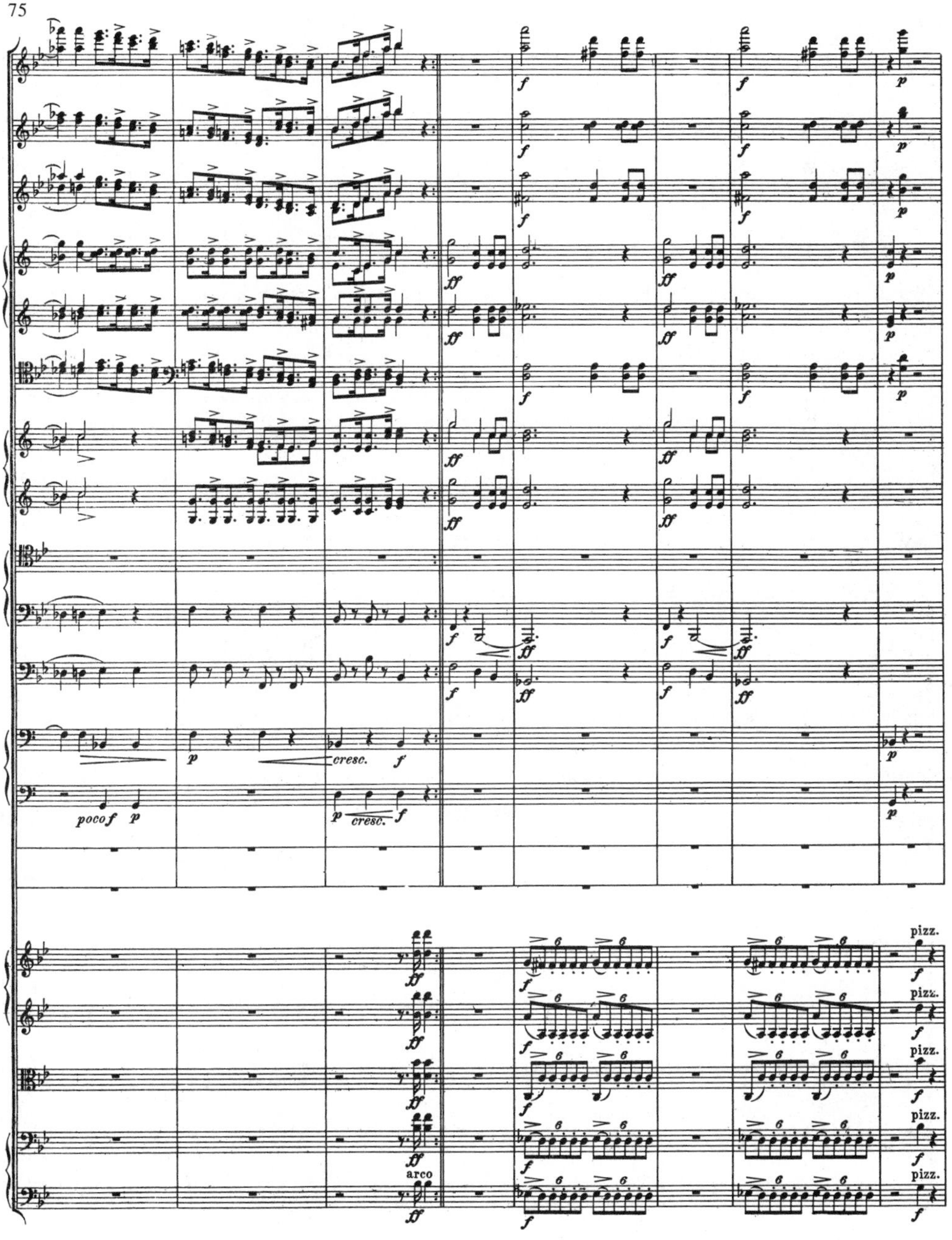
75
cresc.
poco f
cresc.
arco
pizz.

106
a 2.
I.
Soli
Soli
unis.
Soli
Soli
pizz.
arco
pizz.
arco
pizz.
pizz.
arco
pizz.
arco
pizz.
pizz.
arco
pizz.
arco
pizz.
pizz.
arco
pizz.
arco
pizz.
pizz.

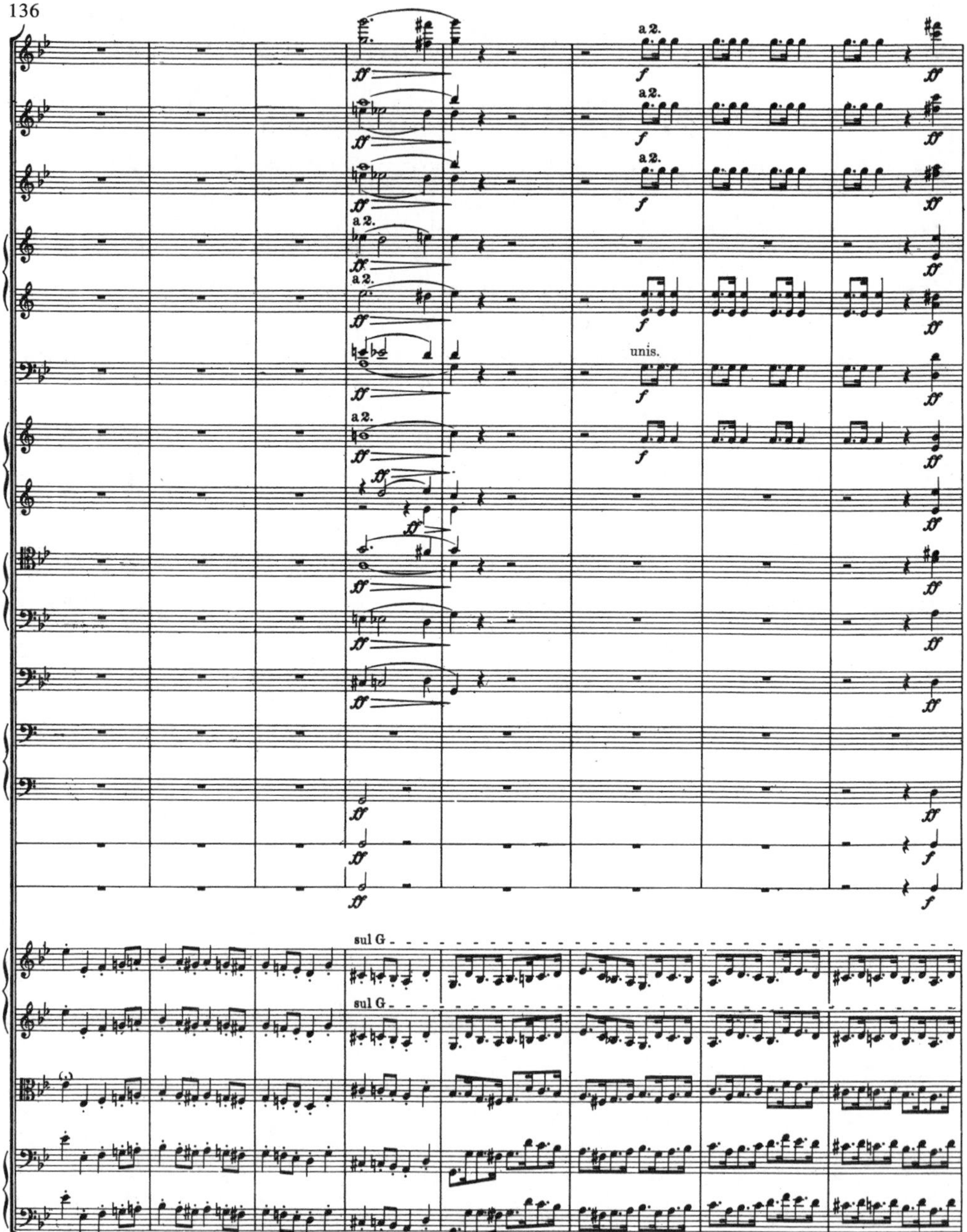
136
a 2.
unis.
sul G

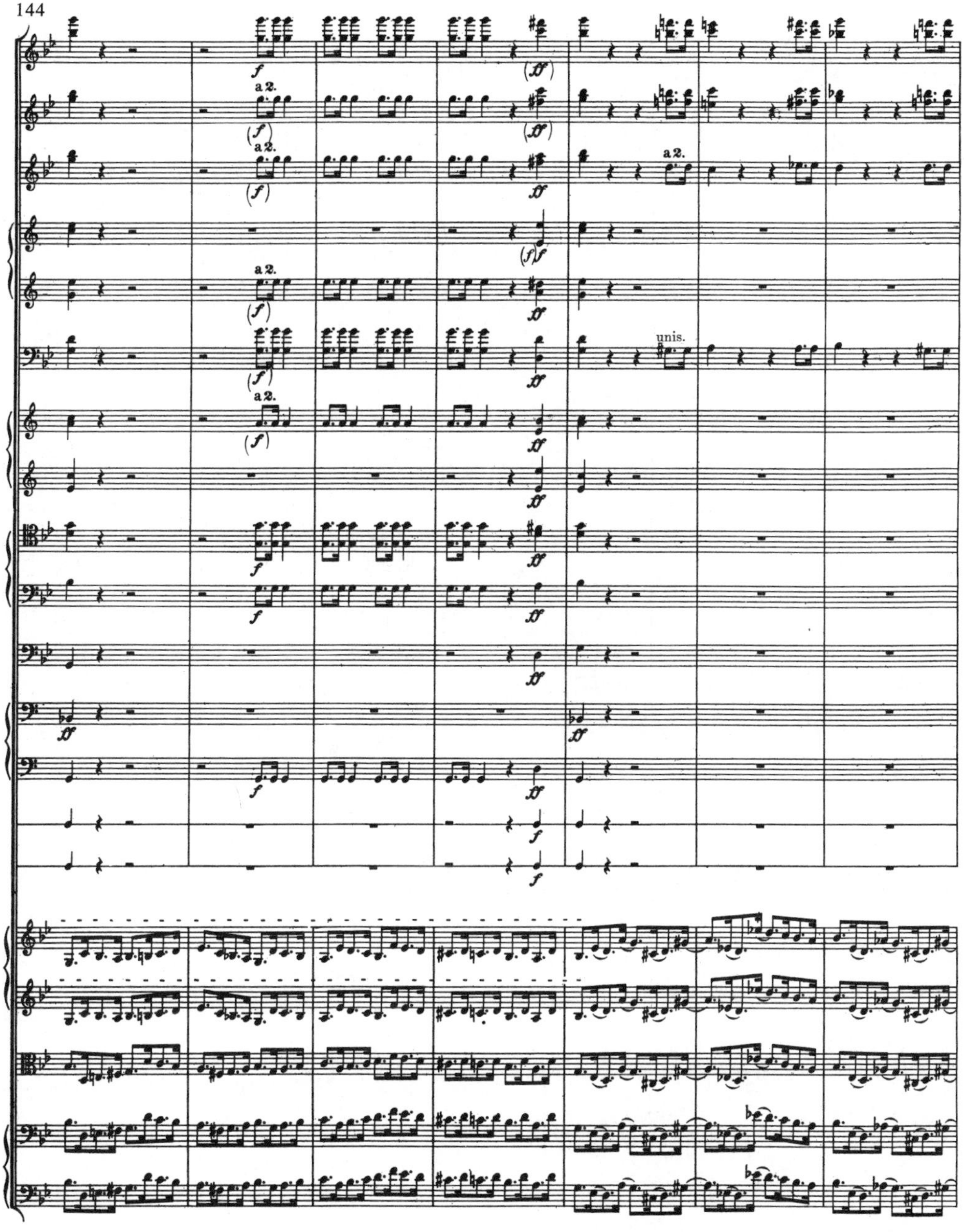
144
a 2.
unis.

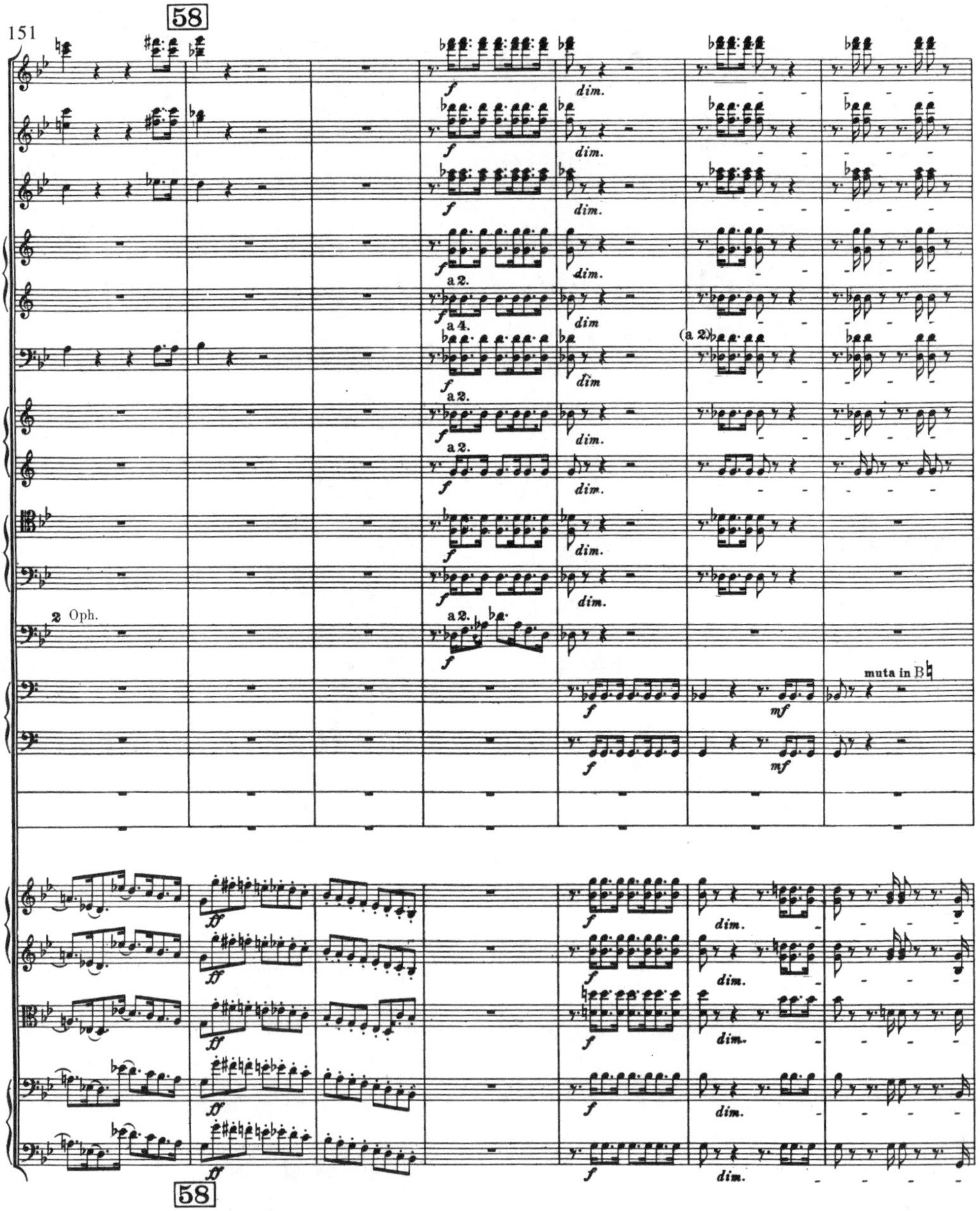
58
151
f
dim.
a 2.
a 4.
(a 2)
2 Oph.
muta in B♮
mf
ff
58

158
a 2.
59
I. Solo
pp dolce assai
ed appassionato
Trois Timbaliers
Three drummers
59

167
rall. poco a tempo
a 2.
I. II.
Fag.
III. IV.
1. Timpanista.
2. Timpanista.
Soli
3. Timpanista.
Tamburo.
Cinelli.
étouffez le son
damp the tone
Gr. Tamb.
étouffez le son avec la main
damp the tone with the hand
pizz.
arco
rall. poco a tempo

V

Dream of a Witches' Sabbath   Songe d'une nuit du sabbat

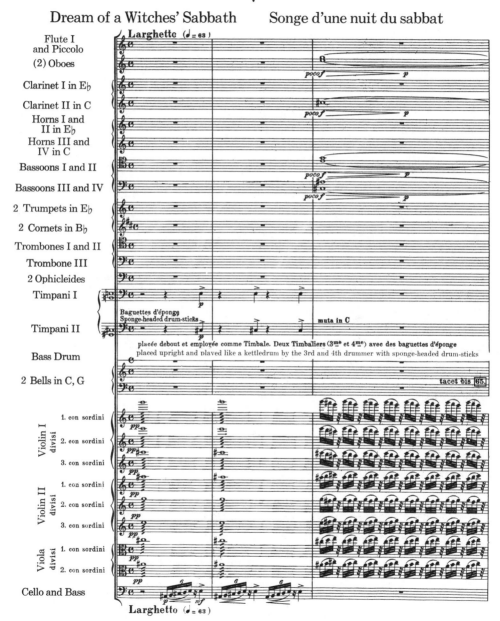

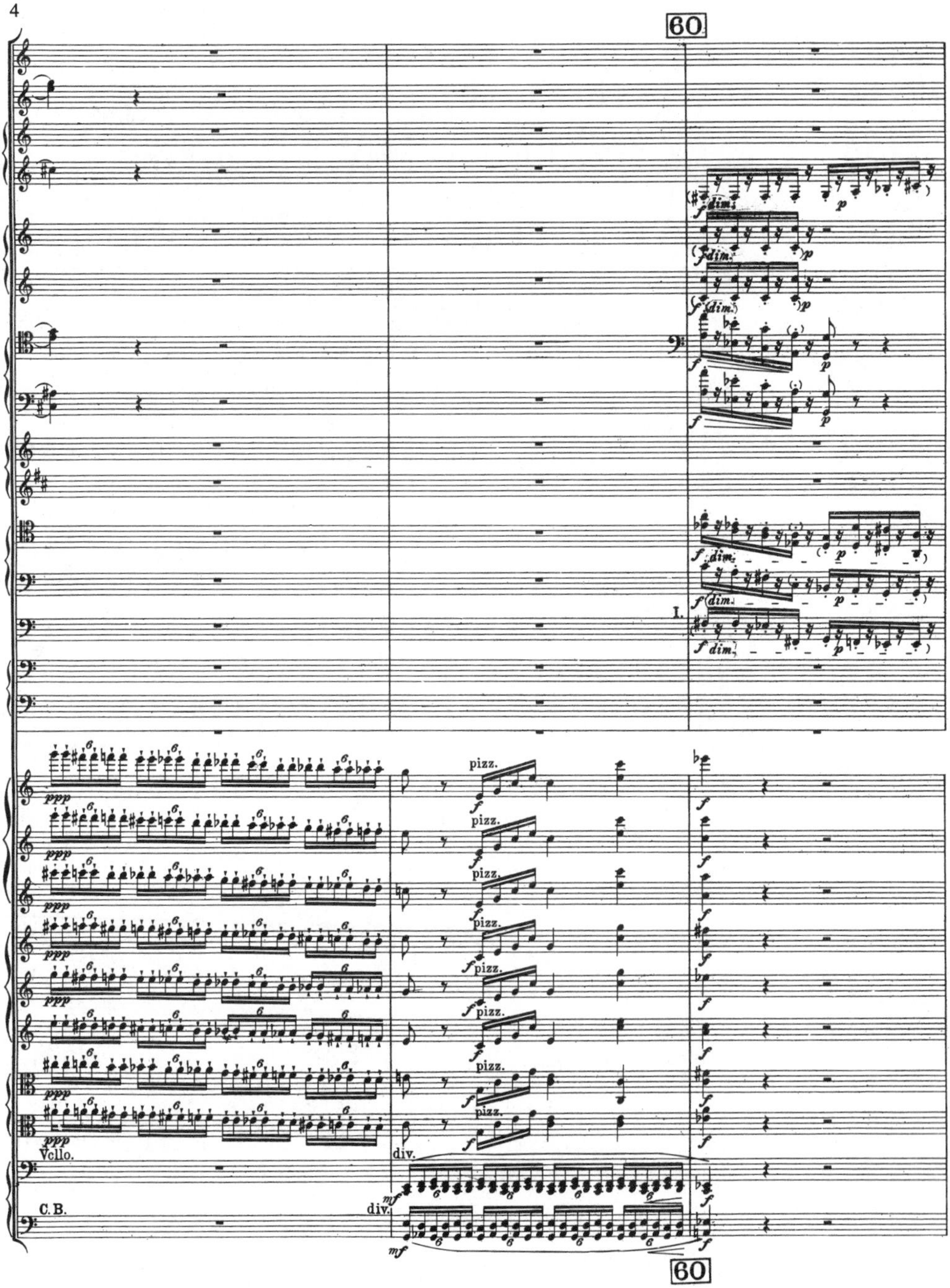
4
60
dim.
I.
pizz.
Vcllo.
div.
C.B.
60

13

21
Allegro (♩. = 112)
Allegro assai (𝅝 = 76)
Solo lointain distant
ppp
tr
cresc.
ff
a 2.
ouvert avec les cylindres
open, with valves
3
I.
p cresc. poco a poco
Sur les deux timbales
p
cresc. poco a poco
sans sourdine
sans sourdine
Allegro (♩. = 112)
Allegro assai (𝅝 = 76)

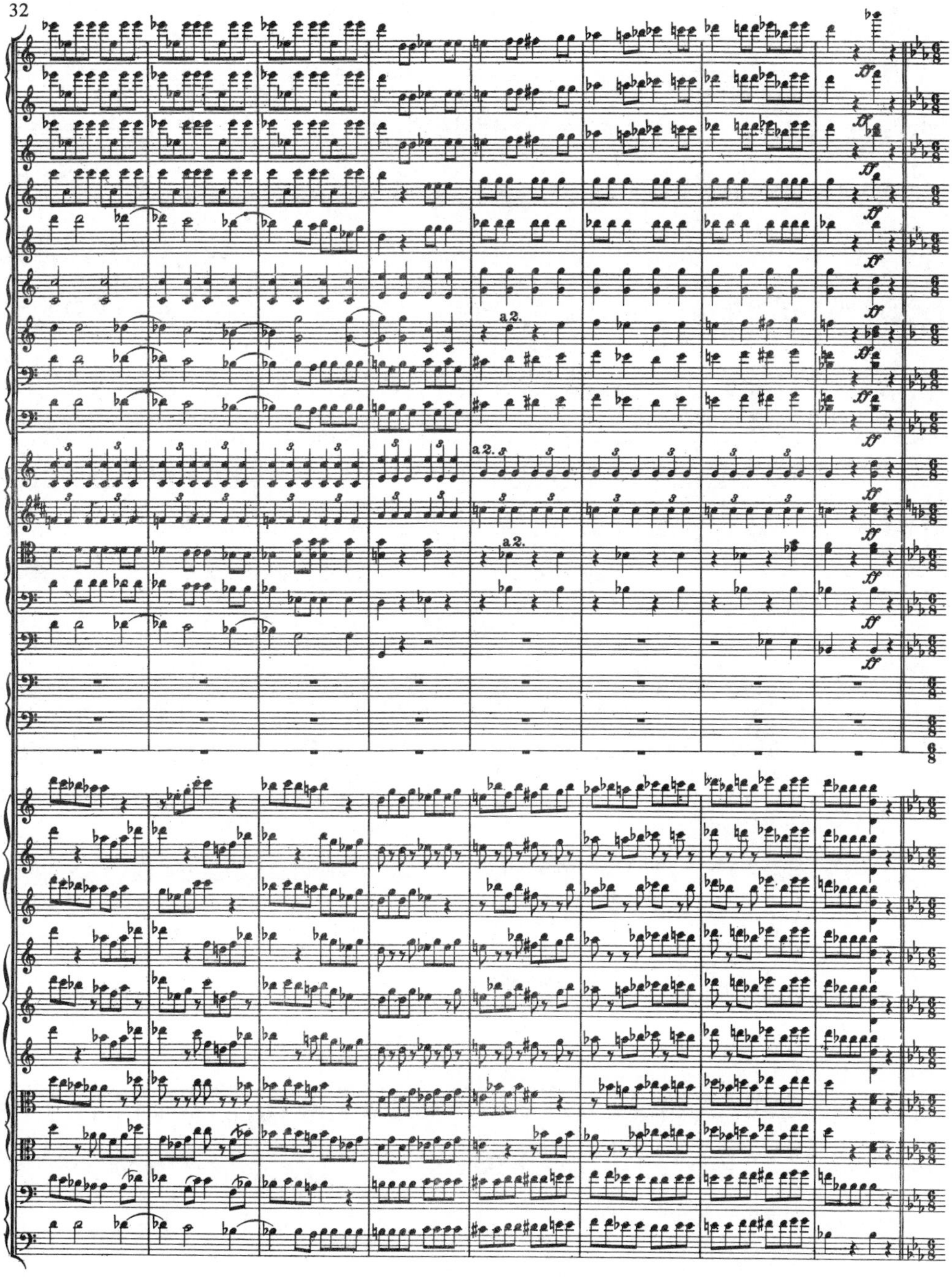
32
a 2.
a 2.
a 2.
ff

67
Fl.
Fl. picc.
Ob.
Clar.
a 2.
Cor.
a 2.
Fag.
unis.
Tr.
Ctti
Tromb.
Oph.
Timp.
Viol.
ff

146
Fl.
Fl. picc.
Ob.
Clar.
Cor.
Fag.
Tr.
Ctti
Tromb
Oph.
Gr. Tamb.
Camp.
pizz.
Viol.
pizz.
pizz.

171

196

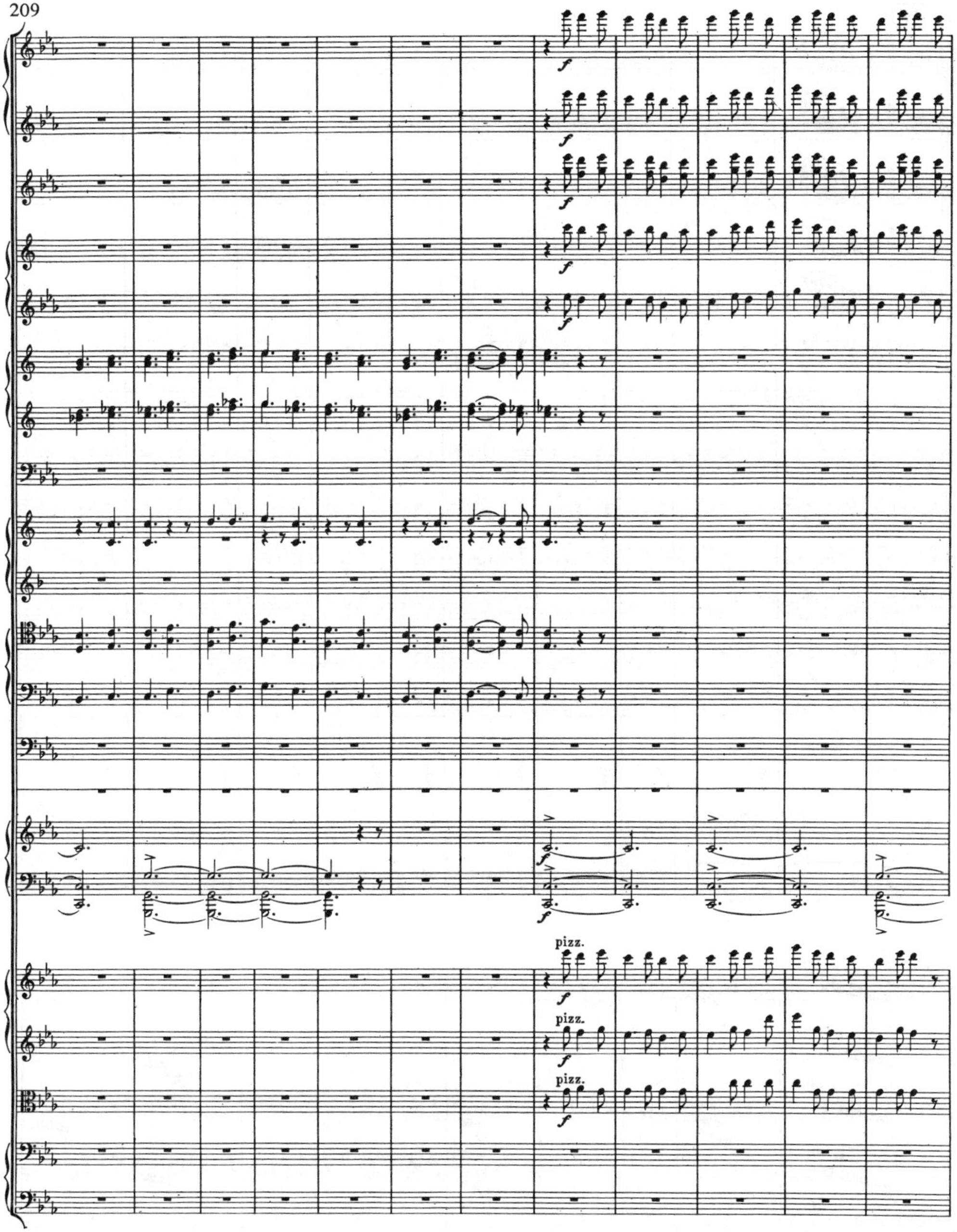
209
f
pizz.

221
69
f
a 2.
a 2.
G-Caisse roulante, deux Timbaliers
mf
Bass-Drum roll, two timpanists
arco
arco
arco
mf
sf
(mf)
69

231
70
Fl.
Fl. picc.
Ob.
a 2
Clar.
Cor.
Fag.
a 4.
Tr.
Ctti
a 2.
Tromb.
Oph.
Baguettes d'éponge
Sponge-headed sticks
Timp.
Baguettes d'éponge
Sponge-headed sticks
Viol.
cresc.
70

Ronde du Sabbat
Witches' round dance

257

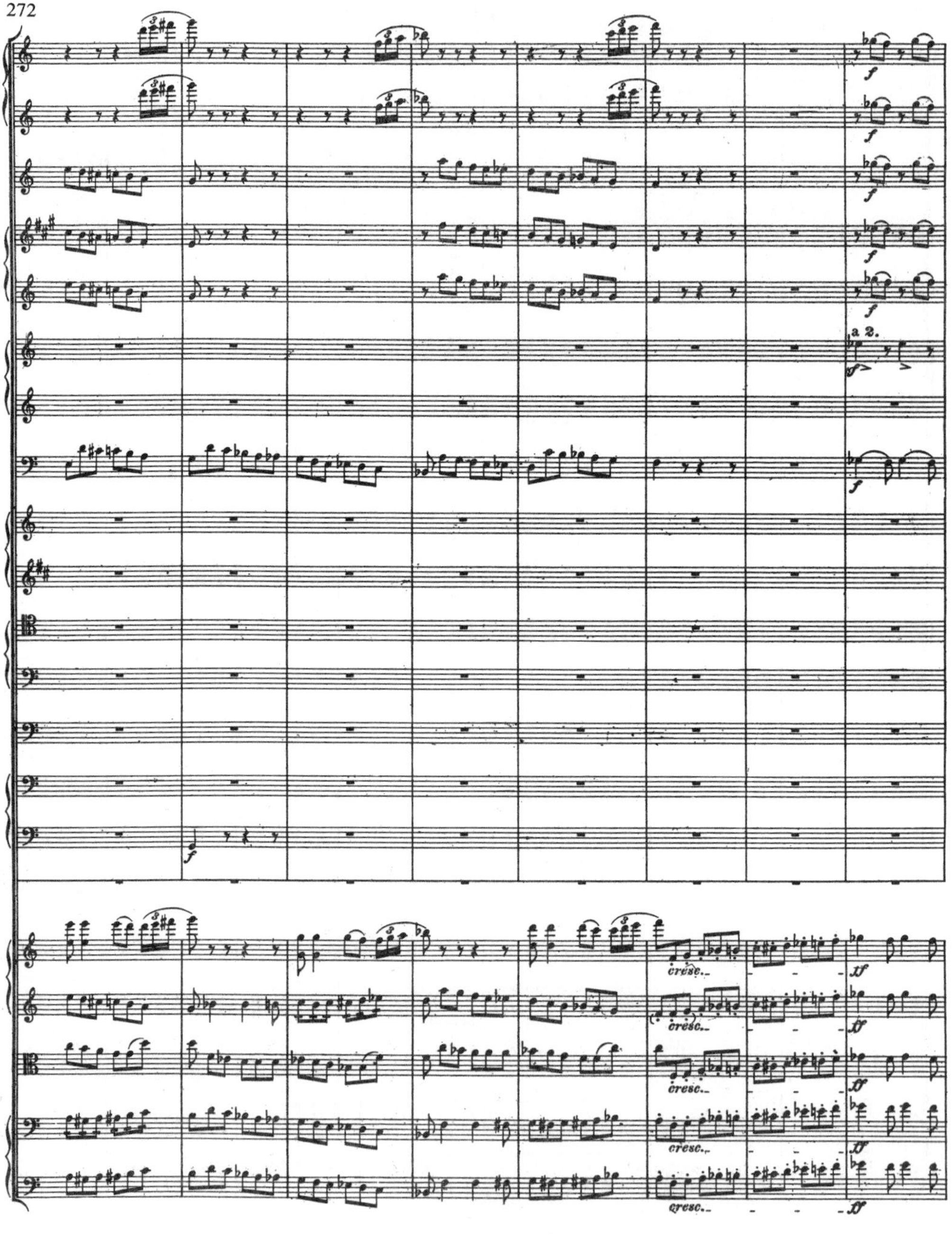
272
a 2.
cresc.

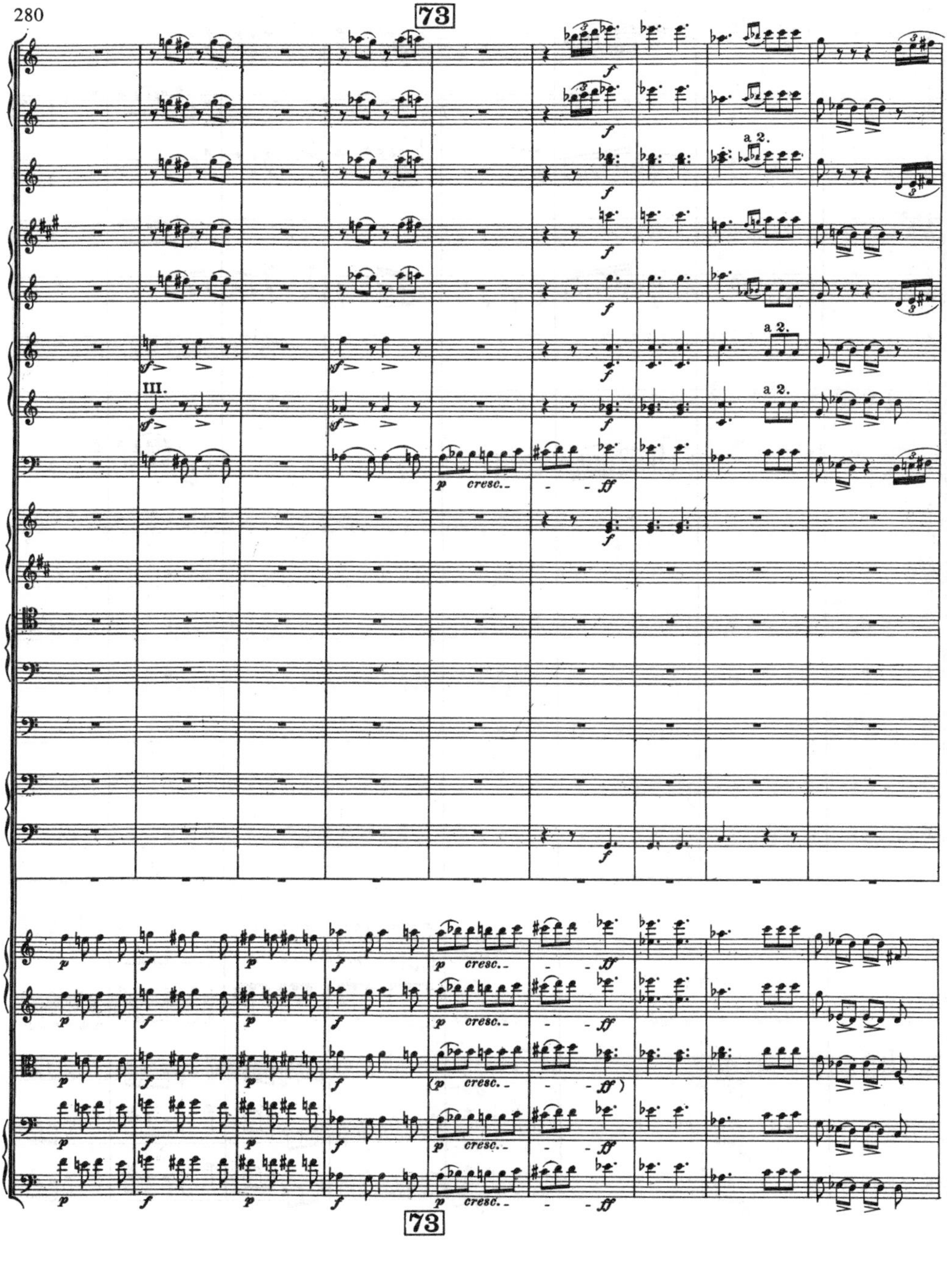
280
73
a 2.
a 2.
III.
p cresc.
f
ff
p
f
(p cresc.
ff)
73

335

345

361
78
cresc. poco a poco
II.
bouché avec les cylindres
IV.
poco sf > p
crescendo
Un Timbalier
One drummer
Solo
pp
cresc. poco a poco
pp
cresc.
Soli
pp
crescendo
78

380

mf
cresc.
I.
cresc. sempre
cresc.
poco a poco
f cresc. sempre
cresc. sempre

Dies irae et Ronde du Sabbat ensemble
414 Dies irae and witches' round dance together

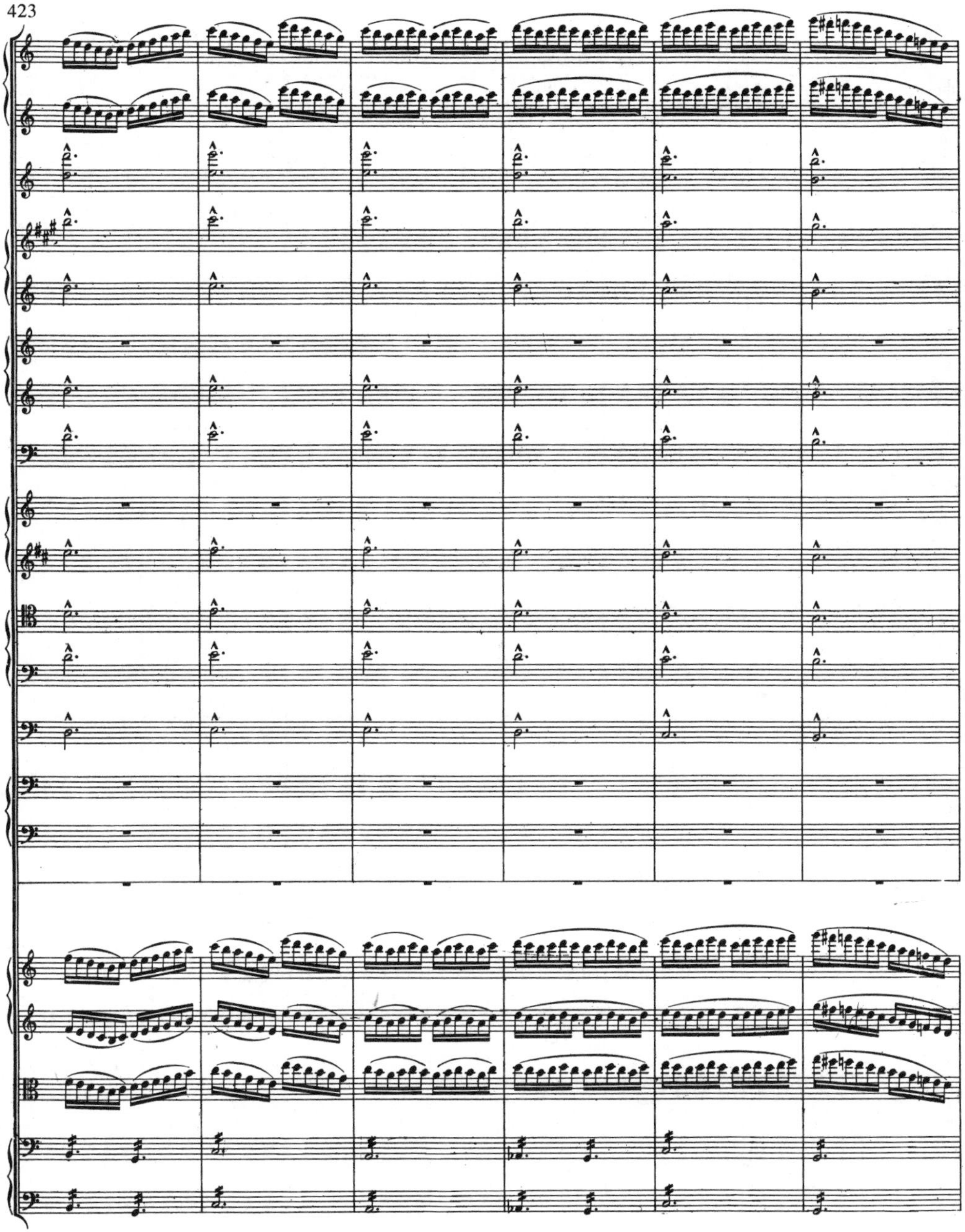
423

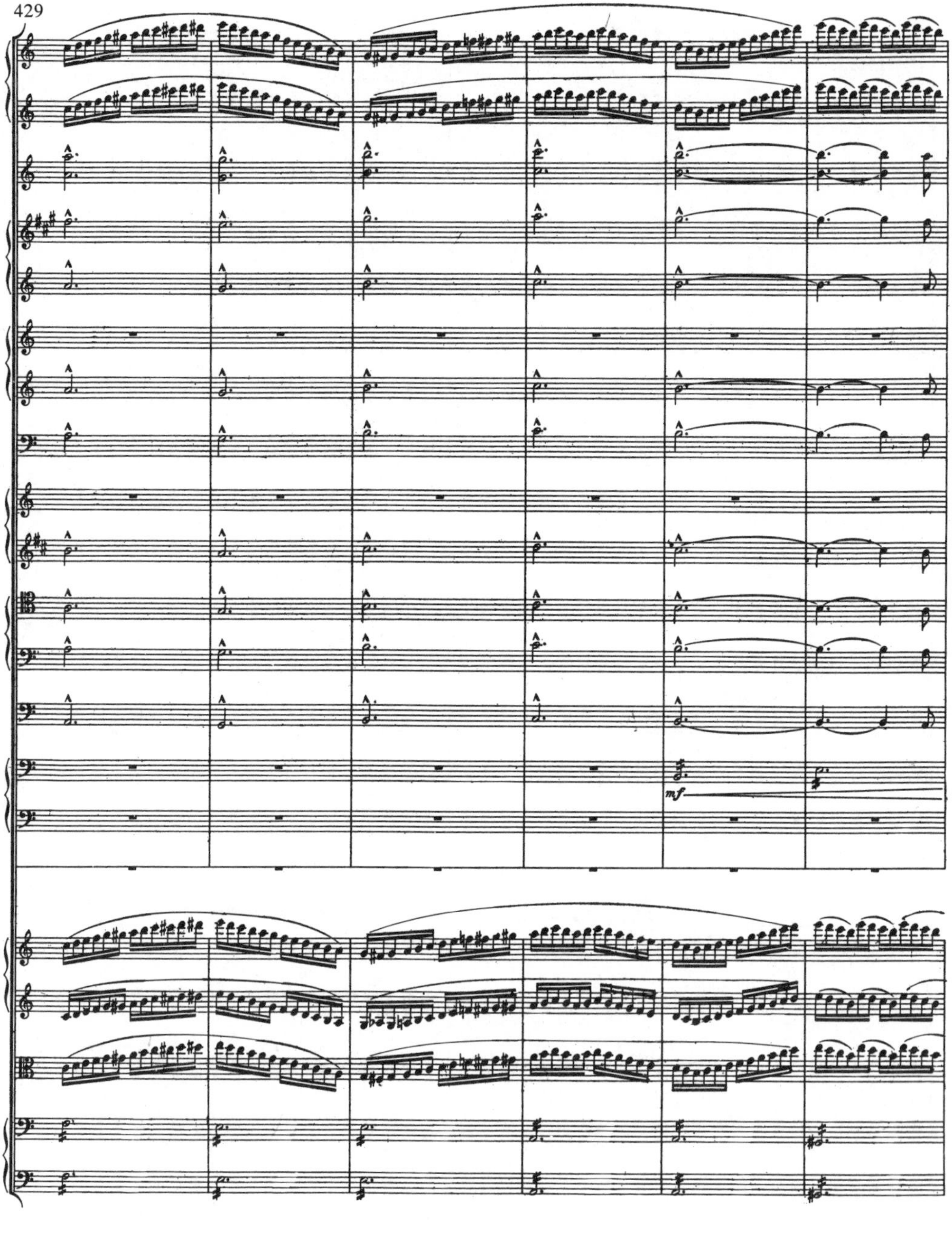
429
mf

441
83
mf
a 2.
mf
mf
unis. mf
frappez avec les bois de l'archet
frappez avec les bois de l'archet
frappez avec les bois de l'archet
(col legno battuta)
mf
div.
83

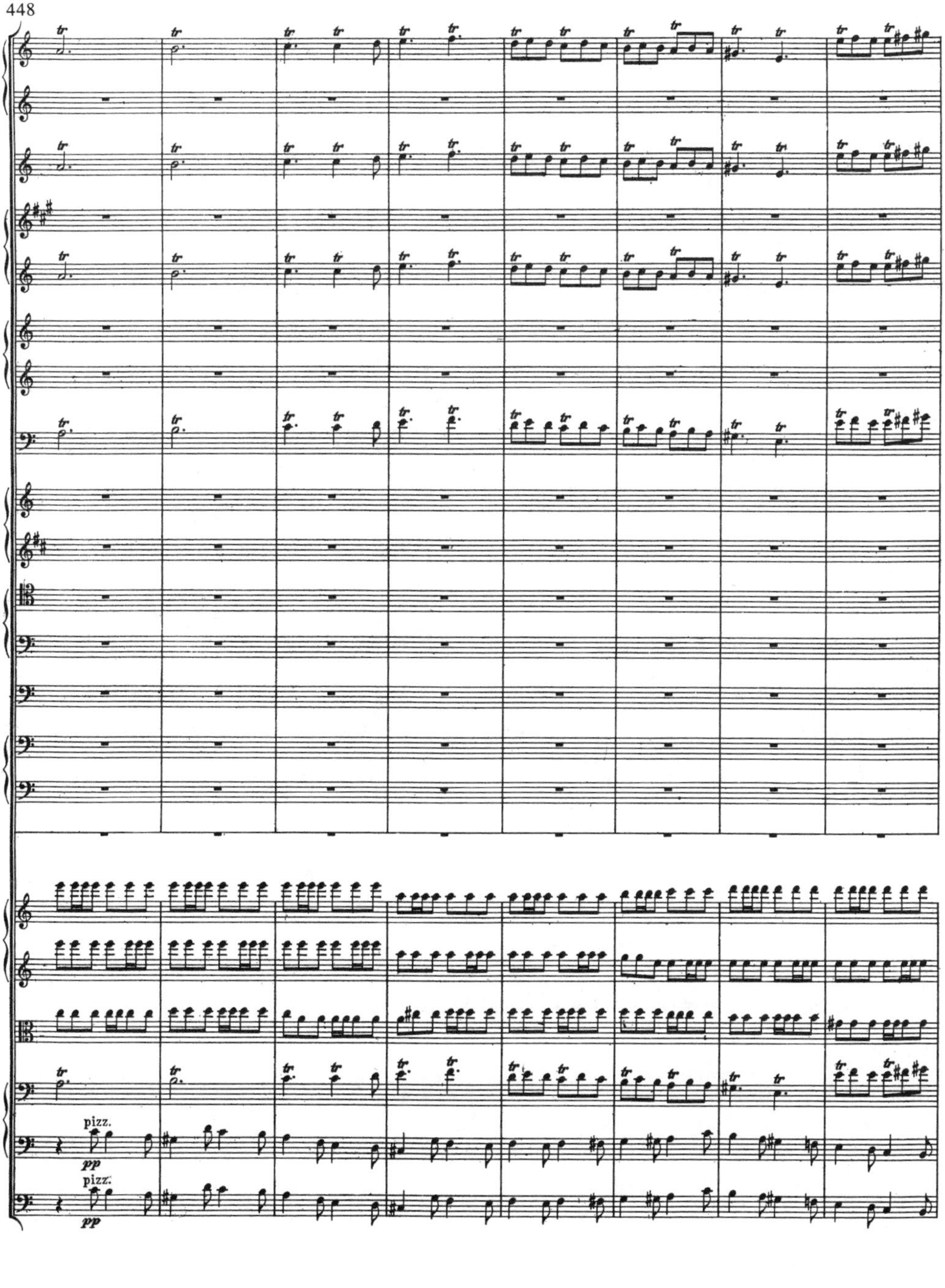
448
tr
pizz.
pp
pizz.
pp

456
Soli
p légèrement
I.
p légèrement
p légèrement
I.
p légèrement
arco

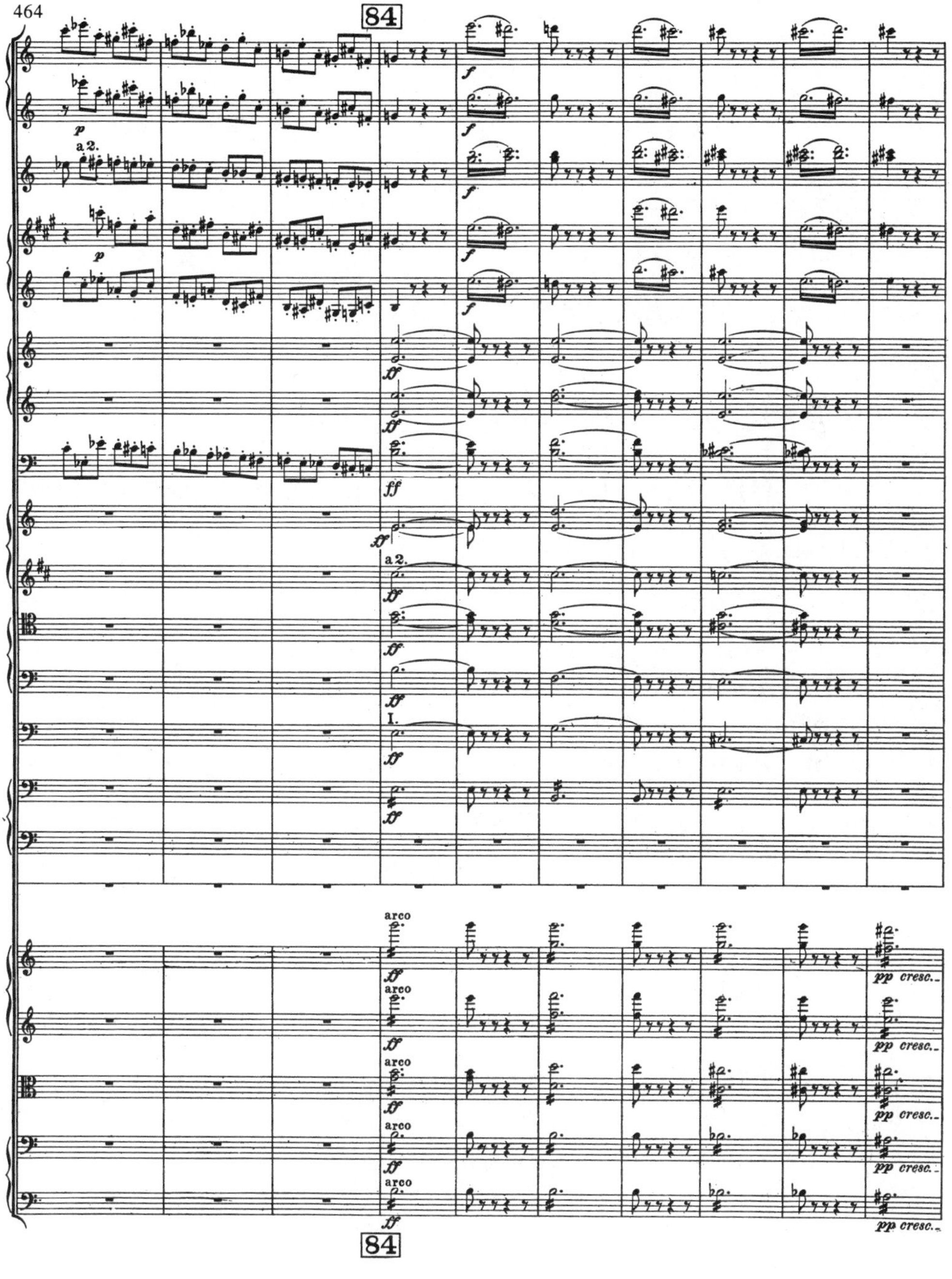
464
84
a 2.
p
f
ff
I.
arco
pp cresc.
84

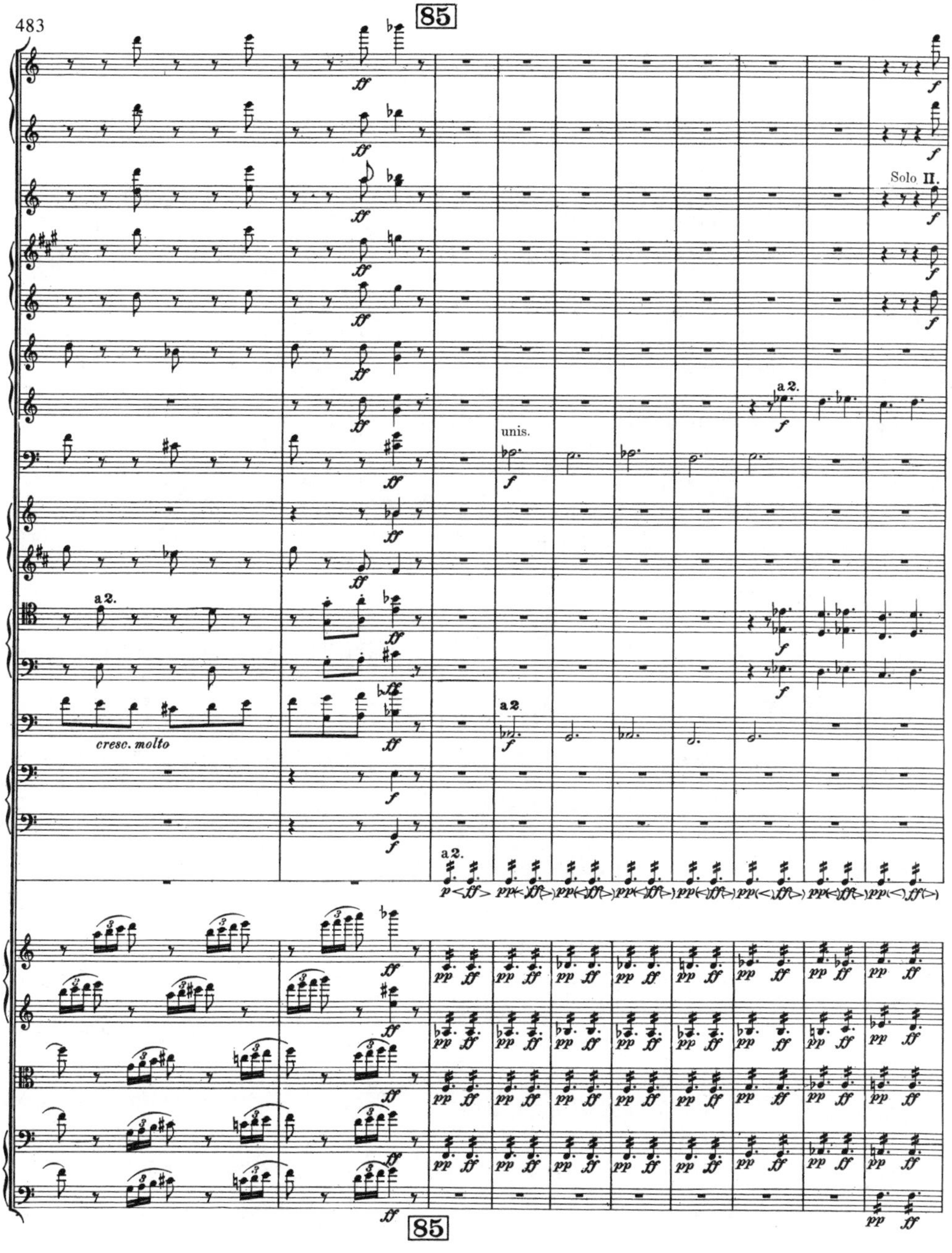
85
483
Solo II.
a 2.
unis.
a 2.
cresc. molto
a 2
a 2.
85

animez un peu

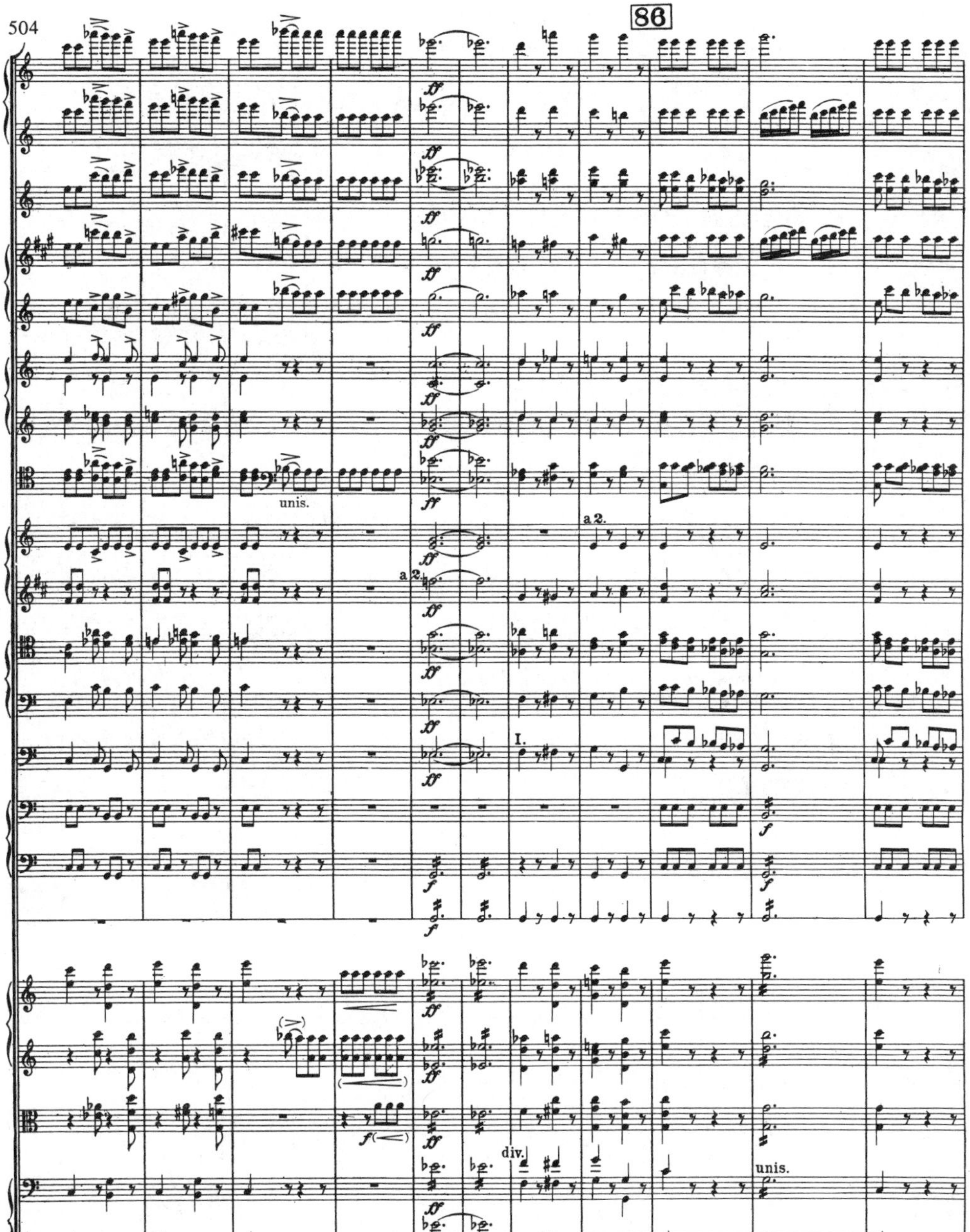
504
86
unis.
a 2.
a 2
I.
div.
unis.
86

515
tenu
unis.
Cinelli.
Coup frappé sur une Cymbale avec une baguette couverte d'éponge ou un tampon
Struck on a cymbal with a sponge-headed drum-stick or a padded stick

Textual Note

The present score is primarily based on the first edition (to be referred to as S). Specifically, I have used two copies in the collection of the Bibliothèque Nationale, Paris, both of which contain emendations in Berlioz's own hand. The first (to be called S_1 when it is necessary to refer to it in contradistinction to the other) is the one Cecil Hopkinson considers an "advance edition," apparently run off by the publisher, Maurice Schlesinger, before the generally available edition of 1845.[1] The second (S_2) is a later printing by Schlesinger's successors, Brandus & Dufour, placed by Hopkinson "after 1858."[2] These have been supplemented by the manuscript (M), also in the Bibliothèque Nationale, and by a set of the original printed parts of 1845 (P), formerly in Hopkinson's own collection, now in the National Library of Scotland.[3]

The present score is essentially S_2, which gives the symphony in its definitive form; the notes call attention to those passages where this version differs substantially from those of the other sources. Berlioz's hand-written emendations have of course been followed. Most of these are corrections of obvious misprints and require no special mention, but there are a few important ones that are pointed out in the notes.

I have drawn on P to fill out missing dynamic marks in the individual parts and to resolve contradictions in the phrasing, etc. (For example, in S there are many cases of slurs beginning at the end of a system but not continued, and of diminuendo signs improperly repeated, rather than continued from one system to the next.) I have used M in the same way, though with much greater caution, since it differs in many respects from the final version. But, since S, P, and M differ widely from one another in phrasing throughout, all such corrections have been restricted to the most obvious and unexceptionable points. Otherwise, for the most part, I have simply accepted the phrasing of S, while pointing out im-

1. Cecil Hopkinson, *A Bibliography of the Musical and Literary Works of Hector Berlioz 1803–69*, Edinburgh, 1951, p. 74, No. 36-A.

2. See p. 19. But Temperley adduces evidence that the musical text of this late publication was printed as early as 1846. See the New Berlioz Edition, XVI, p. 173.

3. *Ibid.*, p. 76, No. 36-C.

portant or interesting variations in the other two sources. In a few cases P or M, even though differing substantially from S, has seemed to me preferable to follow; these are duly noted. All markings not specifically found in one of the sources are in parentheses.

Hugh Macdonald has advanced cogent arguments to support his view that Berlioz's accent mark (➤) is in fact always, or almost always, a short but real diminuendo (➤).[4] I believe that Macdonald's conclusions are too sweeping. It is hard to understand, for example, how such a sign under a single kettledrum-stroke (e.g. IV, m. 67) could mean a diminuendo. It is true that S, in many cases, makes no distinction between an accent and such a diminuendo, but this is by no means the case with M and P. On the authority of these sources, therefore, I have tried to distinguish the two. Any reader who wishes to follow Macdonald, however, need only interpret all the accents as diminuendo signs.

Wherever it seemed possible that a misinterpretation of Berlioz's intentions might arise, I have retained the original wording of his directions, even though it might differ from normal usage today. Hence you will find *animez* at I, m. 441, and *più animato* at I, m. 463, despite the fact that the passages are parallel, because that is the way the composer indicated them. But I have not felt it necessary to follow him if, in a single passage, he marks various instruments *crescendo a poco a poco, crescendo poco a poco, crescendo a poco,* and sometimes even *crescendo poco,* all with apparently identical meaning. Similarly, *en diminuant* and *diminuendo* seem to be used synonymously, especially since a given passage may be marked the one way in S and the other in P.

Occasional quotations are made of relevant passages from Berlioz's own *Grand traité d'instrumentation* (indicated as T). The page references are to the first edition of 1843.

First Movement

passim   Four bassoons were commonly employed in the French orchestras of the period. T, p. 124: "Usually one writes for the bassoons in two parts; but since large orchestras always have four bassoons, one can easily write in four real parts, or, better still, in three—the lowest part being doubled at the lower octave to reinforce the bass." Only in the last two movements, and then only occasionally, does Berlioz allow more than two parts. Elsewhere, as P makes clear, he indicates simply *Premier* and *Deuxième Basson*, leaving it up to the conductor to decide when to use doublings and when to omit them.

In M, neither trumpets nor cornets are used in this movement.

4. "Two Peculiarities of Berlioz's Notation," in *Music and Letters,* L/1 (Jan. 1969), 25–36.

1   The meter, both here and at m. 64, is given as **C** in S, as **¢** in M and P. The most reasonable choice would seem to be **C** here, **¢** at m. 64, but unfortunately none of the sources permits this solution.

  S is inconsistent as to the use of dots and slurs, giving the flute only dots, the horn only slurs, and the other instruments that which appears here. M and P suggest the solution here adopted, although they are not entirely consistent. S gives no dynamic indication to the oboe; the *pp* comes from M; P gives *p*.

3   Viol. I: The first slur originally started at the beginning of the measure. The present version is one of the changes indicated by Berlioz on S₂.

7   Viol. I: The phrasing of this theme in P differs in many details from that in S (which M, on the other hand, resembles). For example, P, always more generous with staccato dots than the other sources, adds these to the detached e♭²'s here; and it divides m. 9 into two equal slurs.

12   C.B.: The crescendo and diminuendo marks are from P. Note here the term *soli*. Berlioz uses *solo* and *soli* to indicate those parts that are to be brought into prominent relief, not necessarily solos in the usual sense of the word.

16   S has Berlioz's usual indication for the removal of mutes, *ôtez les sourdines*, in the middle of the measure for all the strings (except the C.B.). While this makes sense for the violins, it is difficult for the violas and impossible for the cellos. The location of the *senza sord.* directions adopted here comes from P, though the wording, unusual for Berlioz, suggests an editorial emendation. (M is of no help, since this passage is the result of a change in the score.)

17   Here occurs the first of a number of explanatory or cautionary notes written by the composer and printed as part of the score: *Les onze mesures qui suivent sont d'une extrême difficulté; je ne saurais trop recommander aux chefs d'Orchestre de les faire répéter plusieurs fois et avec le plus grand soin, en commençant au changement de mouvement (plus vite) et finissant à la rentrée du thème (Iº. Tempo). Il sera bon de faire étudier leur trait aux 1ᵉʳˢ et 2ᵐᵉˢ Violons séparément d'abord, puis avec le reste de l'Orchestre, jusqu'a ce qu'ils soient parfaitement sûrs de toutes les nuances de mouvement, qui me paraissent ce qu'il y a de plus difficile à obtenir de la masse, avec l'ensemble et la précision convenables.* (The following eleven measures are extremely difficult. I cannot too strongly urge conductors to rehearse them several times, and with the greatest care, from the change in tempo (*plus vite*) to the return of the theme (Tempo I). It would be well to have the first and second

violins study their passage work alone at first, then with the rest of the orchestra, until they are perfectly sure of all the nuances of tempo, which I consider the most difficult thing one can get the whole group to achieve, with the requisite ensemble and precision.)

M adds *pp* after the diminuendo marks in the lower strings; it is not clear whether this is meant to coincide with the entry of the violins.

23 Viol. I: Accents on the 2nd and 4th eighths in P.

50–59 Viol. I: The grace notes are slurred to the next sixteenth in P.

64 It will be seen that Berlioz's arithmetic, as revealed by a comparison of his metronome mark with his note on the change of tempo, is not exact.

72 The phrasing of this theme, both here and at its return, shows many discrepancies among the sources. S is followed here.

105 *Retenu* over the second half of the measure in M and P. From here through m. 109, the markings in P are chaotic, differing between Viol. I and Fl. S is at least consistent.

133–38 M gives a passage to the timpani here.

134–38 Fl., Clar.: The phrasing differs in all the sources. I have retained that of S, even though it is not entirely consistent— but then, none of the sources is.

162 Viola, Vcello.: P gives staccatos to the 3rd and 4th eighth notes.

167 Fag.: M and P have, oddly, a crescendo sign.

168 Viola,Vcello., C.B.: M and P have a crescendo sign.

178 Fl., Ob.: M and P have a crescendo sign (but not Clar.) .

199 Viol., Viola, Vcello.: M and P, although not entirely consistent, have a diminuendo in this measure, with the *p* beginning on the first beat of the next measure.

214 C.B.: A c♯ seems to be needed on the first beat, but none of the sources gives it.

216 M suggests a more natural dynamic, ending the diminuendo in the preceding measure and arriving at *p* at the beginning of this one. P for the most part supports the reading of S given here.

226 C.B. enters here in P, employing in this measure and the next the pattern of m. 228.

270 M has *retenu* in this measure followed by *a tempo* in m. 272, as well as accents in Fl. and Ob., just as in the exposition.

277–80 Another passage of disagreement among the sources as regards phrasing. I have stuck to S, except in the case of Fag. in m. 280. Here S begins the phrase only with the 2nd half note; I have assumed this to be a misprint of the more likely version of M.

303–05 Viol. I: In P, accents on the first note of each of these measures.

321 Viol. II: In P, staccato dots on the 3rd and 4th eighth notes.

322 Viola: In P, staccato dots on the 3rd and 4th eighth notes.

327 Fl., Ob., Clar.: In P, the slur starts at the beginning of the

measure, as at m. 162.

328   Timp.: Berlioz's complete direction here is *Prenez les baguettes à tête d'éponge* (Take the sponge-headed drumsticks), implying that heretofore the timpanist should have been using the more usual heads covered with leather (*peau*). Berlioz always specifically indicates the use of sponge-headed or wooden-headed (*tête de bois*) sticks. T, p. 262: "There are three kinds of drumsticks, the employment of which so changes the nature of the sound of the timpani that it is more than negligent of composers not to designate in their scores which they wish the players to use. The sticks with wooden heads produce a harsh, dry, hard sound, which is scarcely usable except for striking a violent blow, or for accompanying a huge orchestral tumult. The sticks with leather-covered wooden heads are less hard; they produce a less resounding sonority than the preceding, but one still dry nevertheless. In many orchestras these sticks are the only ones used, and this is very unfortunate. The sponge-headed sticks are the best; more musical and less noisy, they should be used more frequently. They give the timpani a dark, velvety sound, which makes the tones very clear and their pitch therefore fully perceptible; and they are useful for many soft or loud shadings in which the other sticks would produce a wretched or at best an inadequate effect." (The usual heads today are of felt.)

In M, here and occasionally elsewhere, Berlioz asks for *sourdines* (muffles) instead of *baguettes d'éponge*; the latter direction never appears in M. The muffle was apparently a piece of cloth wrapped over the drumhead to obtain the requisite softness. (In the Finale, M specifically calls for such a cloth to be placed over the bass drum. See p. 211.)

346   Viola: S gives *canto solo*, which suggests a single viola; but P has the probably correct *soli*.

360   Ob.: P adds *appassionato*.

382–94   Fl., Ob.: Another passage in which phrasing and dynamics differ among the sources and are inconsistent within each. I have again retained the version of S, except at mm. 384–86, where the crescendo-diminuendo sign, beginning only in m. 385, is surely misplaced. Here I have followed P.

410–11   These two measures are compressed into one in M (and consequently in Liszt's transcription).

412   Some of the parts are marked *animez* in P.

412–41   Since M lacks trumpets and cornets in this movement, its orchestration of this passage differs considerably from the definitive version. The eighth-note figuration is lacking in the upper strings, which present the theme in the same rhythm as the rest of the orchestra.

413–15   It is hard to tell whether the signs here are meant as accents or as short diminuendos, for the sources are highly inconsistent. S seems to support the reading given here.

415–29   In M, and occasionally in P, the staccatos in this passage are indicated by strokes rather than by dots.

421–25   Viol. I: In mm. 421 and 423, P has a slur over the 1st three eighths; in m. 425, over the 1st two eighths.

440   Viol. I: P has a slur from the 2nd to the 4th eighth.

525   P contains much more extreme dynamic markings: *pppp* for Ob., Clar., Fag., and Cor. III and IV; *ppppp* for Viol. I.

Second Movement

passim   With regard to the doubling of the harps, T, p. 80: "The effect of the harps becomes . . . all the better, the more there are."
   The cornet part does not appear in either S or P; it was apparently added to M at some point after the completion of the symphony. (See p. 264

38   Viol. I: M phrases this first statement of the theme in whole measures; later statements are less clear but seem to agree with S. P is inconsistent.

43   Composer's note: *Le signe* ⌒ *indique qu'il faut traîner le son d'une note à l'autre.* (The sign ⌒ indicates that one must glide from one note to the next.) This note occurs in M only.

70–72   Strings: In Viol. I, P marks these three measures more fully, *sf* > *p*, but reverts to a simple > thereafter. The remaining parts have only > , except for the first measure of Vcello., which has sf >.

94   All the sources here give $c\sharp^2$-e^2 in Fl. and e^2 in Ob. A comparison with Clar. and Viol. I, and a glance at the voice leading of the passage, make it almost certain that the reading adopted here is the correct one.

108   Harp I: The reading here is from M and P. S gives the r.h. chord as $f\sharp^2$-a^2-d^3, which is surely wrong.

129–56   This passage is the only one in which S_1 (following M) differs significantly from all later editions. The earlier version is given on pp. 203-04. (P follows the standard version.)

131   Fl.: Here I have followed the markings of M and P as more in keeping with other statements of the theme. S has no crescendo sign, but rather a diminuendo sign from the third beat of this measure to the first beat of the next.

156   Fl.: Although P covers this measure with a single slur, it is possible that Berlioz intends to distinguish Fl. from Clar. by the phrasing of S.

Ex. 1.   II, mm. 129-56, first version.

171–73 Viol. I: P comes to *ppp* in m. 171, followed by a crescendo in the next two measures. But this marking is not supported by those in any of the other instruments, and it misses what I take to be the sense of the passage.

205 Harps I and II: Here, and at m. 264, M doubles each part an octave below.

242 Harps I and II: Note how Berlioz has altered the melody. He cites this passage in illustration of the following, from T, p. 77: "When a melody already played by other instruments is to be reproduced by the harp and contains impossible or merely dangerous chromatic passages, it must be adroitly modified by replacing one or more of the chromatically altered notes by others within the harmony."

331–33 Viol. I, Viola: P continues the *sf*, placing it on the second beat of each of these measures; the Viola becomes *ff* in m. 335.

345–46 Viols. I and II: The markings here are from M. S, which has *mf* in m. 345 and no mark in m. 346, misses the sense of the dynamics. (P is similar to S.)

Third Movement

passim Composer's note about the players of Timp. II: *Pour le final ces 3me et 4me Timbaliers iront prendre la grosse caisse, et les 2mes Timbales seront jouées par le 2me Timbalier seul.* In the Finale these third and fourth timpanists will take the bass drum, and the second pair of timpani will be played by the second timpanist alone.

1–9 Ob., C. ingl.: Except for the accent on a^1 in C. ingl. at m. 2, which is taken from M, and the accent supplied in parentheses at m. 5, this is the version of S. M and P contain staccato marks similar to those found in S when the melody returns at m. 175. (M is hardly reliable here, though, since it employs a different notation. See Schumann's Ex. 12 on p. 242 below). The differentiation between the two occurrences of the melody afforded by S seems to me preferable— the first time more sustained and assured, the second time more fragmentary and disconnected.

15, 17, Winds: In these three places the phrasing is taken from P, which
191 is the only consistent source. S slurs the second and third beats of m. 15, nothing at all of m. 17, and the third through the fourth beats of m. 191. M agrees with S at m. 15 but also adds a longer slur from the second through the beginning of the fifth beat; it agrees with P at mm. 17 and 191.

24–29 The phrasing of this passage and its repetitions is highly inconsistent in both S and P. Not only is M, despite certain doubtful measures, almost entirely consistent, but one can also discern how at least some of the problems of S and P might have arisen through careless reading and copying of M, which is carelessly written to begin with. The phrasing here is, therefore, based on my reading of M; but I have recorded all its deviations from S for those who wish to reconstruct that version.

25   Fl., Viol. I: In S the longer slur excludes the final note.

26   Fl., Viol. I: In S the shorter slur ends on f♯^{2}.

27   Viol. I: In S the longer slur excludes the final note.

28   Fl., Viol. I: In S the slur excludes the final note.

38, 40 Fl., Viols. I and II: In S the longer slur excludes the final note.

42   Fl. II, Viol. II: In S the slur excludes the final note.

53   Vcello.: S wrongly places *arco* over the 1st eighth note. M and P give the reading adopted here.

73–76   Viol. I: P divides each measure into two equal slurs.

76   Fag., Viola II, Vcello.: In S, the slur excludes the final note.

77–79   Winds: The phrasing here, from S, could be given a certain consistency by extending the first slur in Clar. by two more sixteenths; or by adopting the reading of M, which unites each group under a single slur. P is even less consistent than S, but generally supports it.

121–24 Clar.: Here is an echo with different phrasing from its original. P avoids this; it uses the same pattern each time (that of S at mm. 135–38). But M, although slightly different from S, strongly suggests that here, at least, the inconsistency is intentional.

131–32 Viol. I: M has staccato dashes instead of dots.

135–38 Winds: Here the echo copies the original phrasing!

141–42 Viol. II: M has staccato dashes instead of dots.

146–47 P divides each measure into two equal slurs. I favor the reading of S given here, but I suspect that Viol. I at m. 147 should be changed to agree with the other parts.

159   Viol. II: S gives c^1 as the last note; M and P give b♭. I have preferred the latter, which creates a rising line to the c^1 in Viol. I in the next measure.

175–93 C. ingl.: We have an additional source here, since this passage was reprinted as an example in T, illustrating the quotation below. On this authority I have supplied the c^2 at m. 175 with a staccato dot. (T supports S at m. 191.) T, p. 124: "In the Adagio of one of my symphonies the English horn, after having repeated at the lower octave the phrases of an oboe, like the voice of a youth answering that of a young girl in a pastoral dialogue, restates the fragments of the melody (at the end of the movement) with a muffled accompaniment of four timpani, while all the rest of the orchestra is silent. The feelings associated with desertion, neglect, and mournful isolation that this forsaken melody evokes in the hearts of certain listeners would not have one quarter of their force if the melody were sung by an instrument other than the English horn." Strange that Berlioz should have so misremembered the beginning of the movement!

188   Timp. II and III: T agrees here with M and P in changing the obviously wrong diminuendos of S to crescendos.

Fourth Movement

passim Berlioz used the C clarinet not for convenience of key, but because of its tone color. T, p. 137: "The C clarinet is harsher than the one in B♭; its voice has far less charm. . . . In general, players ought to use only those instruments designated by the composer. Since each of these instruments possesses its own individual character, it is at least probable that the composer has chosen one or the other of them for this or that tone color, and not out of caprice."

In M, instead of two cornets in B♭ there is a single *trompette à pistons* in E♭; its part is approximately that of Ctt. I. Similarly in the finale, instead of cornets we find two such valve trumpets. In the latter case Berlioz appears to have written *Cornets* at first, then to have scratched out the word and substituted *Trompettes*; elsewhere in the finale he left the word *Cornet* as a place-finder in the score. What this suggests is that the composer preferred trumpets. Later, realizing that in France, at least, the ordinary orchestra would have only two (natural) trumpets and two cornets, he settled for that. In the one case it meant substituting two cornet parts for a single trumpet part; in the other, returning two trumpet parts to the instruments originally designated. Would Berlioz then have approved of those performances today in which all four parts are taken by valve trumpets? T, p. 197: "The cornet is in style in France today, especially in a certain musical world where elevation and purity of style are not considered as essential qualities; it has thus become the indispensable solo instrument for contradances, galops, variations, and other second-rate compositions. Nowadays we are accustomed to hearing it in dance orchestras, playing more or less unoriginal and undistinguished melodies; this fact, and the character of its timbre, which has neither the nobility of the tones of the horn, nor the dignity of those of the trumpet, make it quite difficult to introduce the cornet into a serious melodic context."

M designates alto, tenor, and bass trombones here; S and P change these to alto and two tenors, although in V, m. 238, the part for Tromb. III is still inadvertently designated *Tromb. basse* in S. The most important difference between the original parts and those that replaced them occurs in IV, mm. 62–108. The characteristic pedal tones of the tenor trombones (which, as we shall see, Berlioz was proud to have used) are missing in M. On the bass trombone these pitches either would have to be played normally or else would be completely impossible, depending on the type of instrument used. Perhaps Berlioz came to make a virtue of necessity, for as T, p. 199, says, ". . . Not all orchestras in France have alto trombones, and the bass trombone is almost unknown there." Or perhaps—in view of the fact that the original "bass" part can perfectly well be taken by a tenor—the young Berlioz had been guilty of a mistake that T goes on to censure: "The bass trombone is almost always exchanged for the third tenor trombone, which must assume the performance of the lowest part. On this account it is mistakenly called the bass trombone, from which it differs greatly." (The alto trombone later became obsolete, a fact that creates problems at IV, m. 122.)

The ophicleide was a member of the keyed-bugle family. This family of instruments produced scales by means of holes bored into the sides of their tubes, just as woodwinds do. Until the development of the tuba, the ophicleide was often used, especially in France, as a bass for the brass. T, p. 227: "The timbre of these low tones is rough, but it can do marvels, in certain cases, beneath massed brasses." M uses only one ophicleide, in C; later a second in B♭ was added; it appears only as a reinforcement, doubling other parts at the end of the movement.

In a handwritten note added to S₂, Berlioz gave permission to substitute for the second ophicleide a "tuba in E♭, in which case the part must be transposed down a fourth." The tuba was growing in popularity, especially in Germany. T, p. 196, finds "its timbre incomparably nobler than that of the ophicleides."

Today, of course, both ophicleide parts are entrusted to tubas. For this reason, and to facilitate score reading, they are given here as nontransposing, both in this movement and in the Finale.

In M, the timpani are muffled at the beginning. As he had done in the first movement, Berlioz later called for sponge-headed sticks instead. But by an oversight S retains the direction *sans sourdines* at m. 121, when the wooden sticks are taken up.

1   Again the meter is 𝄴 in S, 𝄵 in M and P.

Composer's note: *On peut, dans ce morceau, doubler les instruments à vent.* (The winds may be doubled in this movement.)

Cor.: The composer's direction refers to the fact that in this movement and the next, he has authorized the use of either natural or valve horns. But even if the latter are used, he still desires here the special color of the hand-stopped tones.

61–62 Timp. I: According to S and M. P has:

62 Cor.: At this point, if valve horns are being played, the valves should be used in order to obtain unstopped tones.

62–77 The distinction between accents and diminuendo marks here is taken from S and M—if I read them aright. These sources are by no means always clear, but it does make sense to differentiate in this way between shorter and longer note values (although such distinctions seem excessive in the case of the timpani). P, on the other hand, preserves the difference only for Fag. and for Cor. I and II; for the other instruments, accents alone are used.

74–77 Tromb. II: Here, and at mm. 101–04, P has Tromb. II doubling Tromb. III.

88 Timp. I: In S, the diminuendo sign is obviously misplaced, coming at the end of the measure.

89–92 C.B.: Here and at mm. 97–100, P changes the bow at the beginning of each measure.

97 Viol. II: The 4th quarter is a[1] in M, f[1] in P, and g[1] in S! Berlioz has corrected it in S$_2$ to f[1].

97–108 In T, after a discussion of the use of trombone pedal tones in his Requiem, Berlioz writes (p. 204): "In another place I have used the pedal tones of the tenor trombone, though with an entirely different aim. I wanted the lower harmonies to sound with extreme harshness, in an unusual timbre. I believe I have achieved this by the fifth of two tenor trombones, and further on by the diminished seventh between an ophicleide and a pedal A of the tenor trombone." He appends a quotation of this passage.

101–02 Viol. II, Viola, Vcello.: In P, those sixteenths that are not slurred are given staccato dots.

114–21 Ob., Clar.: In P, those eighths that are not slurred are given staccato dots, consistently in Clar., less so in Ob. (where there are sometimes dots under the slurs as well). The staccato does not extend to m. 122 in these instruments.

127–28 Tr.: M gives these notes staccato dots as well as ties, suggesting an articulation on each half note.

131–35 P is more generous with staccatos here than the other sources are. For example, in Fag., and C.B., it dots the entire passage from the 4th quarter of m. 132 through the 1st quarter of m. 135. Other staccatos are desultory. I believe that P misunderstood, or forgot, or deliberately changed the sense of the passage. In S, the dots are used only to represent the rests in the original version of the theme; as a result, a heavy, fairly sustained articulation is followed by a contrasting staccato in mm. 135–39.

155   Composer's note: *Il n'y a pas de faute de copie ici; c'est bien l'accord de SOL NATUREL MINEUR qui froisse de très près l'accord de RÉ BÉMOL MAJEUR; l'auteur recommande aux Violons et Altos de ne pas corriger leurs parties en mettant des ♭ aux RÉ quintes de l'accord de SOL.* (There is no misprint here; the G-minor chord really does clash with the D♭-major chord by close proximity. The composer urges the violinists and violists not to correct their parts by flatting the D's, the fifths of the G chord.)

170–78   Fag. III and IV: In P the lower octave is missing, the instruments taking the upper note in unison.

The snare drum is missing in M and S_1.

Fifth Movement

passim S_2 contains a handwritten note by Berlioz recommending the use of the D♭ piccolo, with the appropriate transposition of the part. This was an instrument used in military bands; it sounded a half tone higher than the normal piccolo. It is not clear why Berlioz wished to make the substitution; at any rate, he changed his mind, since the note has been scratched out.

In P, Cor. I and II stand in C and are given the parts here assigned to III and IV. Conversely, Cor. III and IV are in E♭, and take the parts of I and II here.

Originally the cornets stood in E♭. But a handwritten note in S_2 states: "The cornet part must be re-engraved at the transposition for the key of B♭." This in fact had already been done in P, as a further note points out. A probable reason is given in T, p. 193: "The best cornets, those that I believe should be used almost exclusively, are the cornets in G, and especially those in A♭, A, and B♭. The lower keys, such as those of D, E♭, E, and even F, are generally poor in tone color and lack precision of intonation." It is interesting that in his revision of the treatise in 1855 Berlioz removed the G cornet from the approved group and placed it in the other; yet he retained this instrument in the first movement of the symphony.

In M, the second ophicleide part is taken by a serpent. This was a cross between woodwind and brass—a wooden body with a metal mouthpiece—that was already out of general use, except in churches. T, p. 230: "The essentially barbaric sound of this instrument was much better suited to the rites of the bloody religion of the Druids than to those of the Catholic Church, where it is still to be found. . . . One must allow an exception only for the use of the serpent in the Requiem to double the terrifying plainchant of the *Dies irae*. Then its cold and repulsive howling is doubtless appropriate. . . ."

The old name of the bass drum, "long drum," shows that its shape was different from the one familiar today. It was an elongated cylinder, so that when Berlioz directs that it should be placed upright, he means it to be stood on one of its heads. T, pp. 275–76: ". . . In a symphony, in order to maintain a muffled roll, much lower than that available from the lowest range of the timpani, I have had this performed by two timpanists playing simultaneously on one bass drum, standing erect like a military drum." In M, the drum is to be "covered with a cloth." Here again, the sponge-headed sticks replace the muffle.

6   Fag.: Here and at m. 11, P unites Fag. I and II on the upper part, III and IV on the lower. (M gives no indication.)

9   Cor.: Compare the direction here and at mm. 19, 370, and 372, with the one at the beginning of the preceding movement. There, the use of valves was forbidden so as to make sure of getting stopped tones. Here, their use is enjoined—again in order to produce the stopped timbre. (On a natural instrument, the C's would be available only as open notes.) M calls for mutes here, but nowhere in the definitive version of the symphony are muted horns to be found. Berlioz evidently came to distrust them; they are not used in his mature works, nor are they mentioned in T.[5]

18–22   Strings: The directions to remove the mutes are from P. They are lacking in S, no doubt because they were inadvertently omitted from M when part of this passage was revised.

27   Clar. II: S has f^1 as the first note of the measure, which is clearly a misprint. Both M and P have g^1.

29   The metronome mark of 67 in S is surely a misprint for 76. (M and P give no metronome marks.)

40   On the use of the E♭ clarinet here, T, p. 137: "The small E♭ clarinet produces piercing sounds, which from high A on up can very easily sound coarse. In a recent symphony it has been used just so to parody a melody, to degrade it, to vulgarize it, if one may use such an expression. The dra-

5. On this subject, see Tom S. Wotton, *Berlioz: Four Works*, London, 1929, p. 22.

matic sense of the work required this strange transformation."

57–64 Viola, Vcello.: In P, a crescendo through these measures.

81 Composer's note on the meter: *Ces deux temps* ₵ *sont égaux à ceux de la mesure à* $\frac{6}{8}$. (These two beats of ₵ are equivalent to those of a measure of $\frac{6}{8}$).

101 There was originally a double bar at the end of this measure. It is scratched out in S_2 by Berlioz, who calls for its replacement by a single bar line.

102 Composer's note: *Si l'on ne peut trouver deux Cloches assez graves pour sonner l'un des trois UT et l'un des trois SOL qui sont écrits, il vaut mieux employer des Pianos. Ils éxécuteront alors la partie de Cloche en double octave, comme elle est écrite.* (If bells cannot be found that are deep enough to strike one of the three C's and one of the three G's written here, it is better to use pianos. In that case they will play the bell part in double octaves, as it is written.)

241 Composer's note: *Le mouvement, qui a dû s'animer un peu, redevient ici, comme à la lettre A, No. 104 =* ♩. *(Allegro).* (The tempo, which has had to speed up a little, returns here to that of [No. 63:] Allegro, ♩. = 104.)

269 Viola: S gives the 3rd eighth as g[1]. M and P both have f[1], which agrees with the sequence at m. 271.

444 On the use of *col legno*, T, p. 20: "In a symphonic movement that mingles the horrible with the grotesque, the bowsticks are used for striking the strings. This bizarre method should be very rarely employed, and must be well motivated; moreover it produces a perceptible effect only in a large orchestra. . . ."

480–84 Oph.: In M, the part is much simpler here; the ophicleide takes only the first and fourth beats of each measure, and the serpent is silent.

512 Fag.: Here and in mm. 514, 516, and 518, P gives the first beat of each measure as a unison middle C. M agrees with S.

513 Fl., Picc., Clar. I: Here and in mm. 515, 517, and 519, M and P extend each slur through a full half-measure.

520 Viol. II: P adds staccato dots, but only for one measure.

ANALYSIS

Unless specified otherwise, all numbered footnotes in the following
essays are those of the authors.

Two Contemporary Critiques

FRANÇOIS-JOSEPH FÉTIS

Critical Analysis †

Episode in the Life of an Artist
Grand Fantastic Symphony by Hector Berlioz
Opus 4
Piano-Score by Franz Liszt

Today François-Joseph Fétis (1784–1871) is perhaps best remembered for his monumental *Biographie universelle des musiciens* and his *Histoire générale de la musique.* In the nineteenth century this Belgian-born musicologist, theorist, critic, pedagogue, and composer, was one of the most influential figures on the Parisian musical scene. His personal relations with Berlioz fluctuated between periods of open warfare and armistices of cool mutual respect. His opinions of Berlioz's music were equally changeable, and it is not always possible to determine which was cause and which was effect.

A great deal of Fétis's power accrued from his position as founder and editor of the *Revue musicale.* The present article appeared in the issue of February 1, 1835; it was a review of the symphony, based on the piano transcription by Franz Liszt. (The transcription was published in 1834 by Maurice Schlesinger, who was later to publish the full score. Note that at this point the symphony was designated as *Oeuvre 4me,* or Opus 4.) The critique is interesting not only for the insight it affords us into one of the most brilliant academic minds in recent musical history, but also for its clear presentation of what persisted, up to our own day, as the accepted opinion of Berlioz: an eccentric genius, insufficiently trained, lacking in melodic and harmonic gifts, but an original orches-

† From *Revue musicale,* Feb. 1, 1835. Translation by the editor.

trator whose innovations later composers could put to better use. Yet the
chief importance of the article lies not in itself, but in the reply which,
as we shall see, it elicited from a far profounder musical intelligence, that
of Robert Schumann.

I remember one day (about twelve years ago) when I was a member of
the examining jury for the composition classes at the Conservatory.
Among the students who brought examples of their work was a young
man who seemed quite bored with the whole proceeding. He showed me
some monstrosity that he believed to be double-counterpoint: it was
nothing but a tissue of harmonic horrors. I made a few corrections and I
explained the reasons for them to the young man in question. His sole
response was to inform me that he held all studies in great contempt, and
that he considered them completely useless to a man of genius. This confession of faith was greeted with great anger by the director of the
Conservatory[1] and some of my colleagues; as for me, I took a different
tack and said to the young man that such musical knowledge was benefi-
cial only to those who knew how to use it and realized its purpose. Those
who mistrusted it could make no progress in their studies, which would
be useless to them. I then advised the young calumniator of counterpoint
and fugue to give up subjects that he valued so little and to put himself
at the free disposal of his genius, if he had any. He followed my advice,
left the Conservatory, and from that very day began to play his role as
reformer of music. That young man was M. Berlioz.

During the same period he assembled a good number of musicians at
the Church of St. Roch to perform what he called a Mass; everyone came
away shrugging his shoulders and saying that what he had heard was not
music.[2] I know that such judgements are often lightly put forward about
works heralding profound changes in artistic style, so I did not allow
myself to become prejudiced against M. Berlioz.

Some time later he arranged to have a rehearsal of some new prod-
ucts of his pen.[3] Chance led me to the small concert hall of the Conservatory while it was going on. They were playing, I believe, an overture; the

1. Then Luigi Cherubini (1760–1842), who was director from 1822 until his
death. This whole account is somewhat suspect. For one thing, Berlioz did not enter
the Conservatory until 1826; furthermore, he continued to study there until winning the Prix de Rome in 1830. [*Editor*]

2. This refers to the performance on July 10, 1825, of Berlioz's Mass, which had
been commissioned by the choirmaster of St. Roch. The composer subsequently
destroyed the work as an unworthy product of his immaturity. See *Memoirs*, pp.
54–58. [*Editor*]

3. Probably for the concert of May 26, 1828, at which were performed two overtures and some vocal works. Fétis's account of the rehearsal is borne out by Berlioz's
own. See *Memoirs*, pp. 98–103. [*Editor*]

orchestra was bursting with laughter while trying to perform. At each repetition of a passage another instrument would be missing, for everyone was slipping out. Finally it became impossible to realize the composer's intentions, and the rehearsal was over. What I had just heard was horrible, and I had perceived that M. Berlioz was ignorant of certain elements of solfège, let alone composition. Still, there were flashes of quite piquant orchestral effects which convinced me that the head that had conceived them was not entirely empty; I considered it only proper to postpone any judgement thereon. You can see that I was exceedingly patient and conscientious with M. Berlioz.

At last came the day when M. Berlioz gave a concert to let us hear his compositions; it was, I believe, about eight years ago that the concert took place—there have been many others of the same kind since then.[4] The audience at that one was small, and there was scarcely anyone in the hall who was not either a friend or a guest. It was here that we heard for the first time the *Fantastic Symphony*. The audience thought it was having a nightmare during the whole performance; but they did notice the *Marche du supplice* for its novel effects and applauded it. From this moment I began to form my opinion of M. Berlioz: I saw that he had no taste for melody and but a feeble notion of rhythm; that his harmony, composed by piling up tones into heaps that were often monstrous, was nevertheless flat and monotonous. In a word, I saw that he lacked melodic and harmonic ideas, and I came to the conclusion that he would always write in a barbarous manner; but I saw that he had an instinct for instrumentation, and I thought that he might perform a real service by discovering certain combinations that others could use better than he.

Although M. Berlioz was aware of my opinion of his works, he trusted me to the extent of turning to me on various occasions, for he had concluded that I favored encouraging artists and letting them go their own way. Thus he came to see me more than once to ask my help in removing the obstacles he was encountering. As a result, I got M. Lubbert to agree to a performance of his composition on Shakespeare's *Tempest*; I succeeded in conquering the prejudices of those who were opposed to allowing him to enter the Institute competition; and I took steps, at his request, to get his allowance paid to him without his having to go to Italy, for I foresaw that in his state of mind the trip would do him no good—as events have since confirmed.[5]

4. Actually it was less than five years before, since he is referring to the concert of Dec. 5, 1830. [*Editor*]

5. Émile-Timothée Lubbert was the director of the Paris Opera; Berlioz's Fantasy on *The Tempest* (which later became part of *Lélio*) was included in a program there on Nov. 7, 1830. See *Memoirs*, p. 128. The Institut de France ran the com-

After having thus maintained a benevolent attitude toward a self-educated artist whose perseverance in the achievement of his purposes seemed to deserve success, the time has now come for me to change my role and to assume that of critic, in the strictest interpretation of that word, for matters are now very different. The time is past when I had to support M. Berlioz against the unanimous scorn of a famous academic institution, against the public, and against my own distaste; today M. Berlioz poses as an innovator whose doctrines have triumphed and whose enemies are defeated. When he became a journalist, he tried to seduce his readers in four newspapers and periodicals of widely varying political complexions[6]—to seduce them, I won't say to his new musical religion (for so far he hasn't shown us its tenets, except possibly those of barbarity and irrationality), but to faith in his authority. He has friends, whom he has been careful not to choose from the ranks of musicians, except for two or three sincere or hypocritical enthusiasts; and these friends, some of whom are men of importance, praise him to the skies and will probably succeed in convincing the powers that be that M. Berlioz is the genius of the century. You can realize that such a man has no further need of my indulgence; indeed, that would even wound him. In a position of firm resolve he awaits my criticism, for now one can see from the tone he uses that he is judging his judges.

It has always been my desire that M. Berlioz should be presented to a public composed, not of his friends and disciples, but of that enlightened segment of society that instinctively arrives at a sound verdict. The broad daylight of publication seems to me what is needed above all to put to an end the vain quarrels and petty triumphs of coteries; so many premature reputations have since been dispelled when the works themselves have beeen exposed to the sun! It will be the same, I think, with M. Berlioz. To make sure of that, I would say to the directors of all our musical theaters: get M. Berlioz to compose operas great and small, and mount them luxuriously, so that he can have no complaint on nonmusical grounds. To the publishers I would say: buy all M. Berlioz's manuscripts and publish them; let him enjoy all his glory before the world instead of having to solicit the praise of his friends or to praise himself. Perhaps it would be difficult for me to persuade the music publishers and the opera directors that it would be to their advantage to follow my advice; fortunately M. Berlioz himself has taken the trouble to grant one

---

petitions for the Prix de Rome. When Berlioz won, he tried in vain to get permission to stay in Paris (to pursue his courtship of Camille Moke). [*Editor*]

6. Among others, *Le Correspondant, L'Europe littéraire, La Gazette musicale de Paris, Le Journal des débats politiques et littéraires.* [*Editor*]

of my wishes by publishing that famous *Fantastic Symphony*, the foundation of his private success. By means of this publication, everyone can test for himself my judgements as to the merits of the work. I shall try to summarize my opinions in a few words.

Attached to the symphony is a program explaining the subject of each of its five movements. I have already observed several times that such programs derive from the narrowest possible interpretation of the purpose of music, for the full power of this art to affect our feelings is due to its essential vagueness and indeterminacy. I shall therefore not inquire whether each section agrees with the outline of the composer's program, because I know that music cannot express what he has demanded of it, and because I see in this demand one of the causes of the poor results he has obtained.

The first movement is entitled *Reveries—Passions*. There are certain people who often seem to be deep in thought and who, on being asked the subject of their meditations, reveal that they are in fact thinking of nothing at all. I greatly fear that it is the same with the reveries of M. Berlioz, and that they are but empty daydreams; for in this long piece—twenty-two pages of piano score—there are nothing but harmonic monstrosities, devoid of charm or excitement. Not a single melodic idea is thrown onto this pile of confusion, unless one bestows the name *melody* upon a flat, insipid statement recurring several times during the course of the symphony and called by the composer his *idée fixe*.

The second movement (the *Ball*) is less barbarous; but that's all one can say for it. The principal subject is a waltz based on a vulgar theme; for, note well, M. Berlioz falls into triviality as soon as he becomes intelligible. His warmest friends dare not defend him with regard to melody and admit that his music contains little. But how could he compose any? He doesn't know what a musical period is, except, as I have just said, when he writes a vulgar one. Search all the movements of the symphony, and you will see that something is missing from either the antecedent or the consequent of each period, so that the phrase rhythm is constantly halting or crude. No less faulty, in every period of the symphony, is the sense of climactic progression, so lively and so compelling in the music of the great masters; M. Berlioz has no idea of what it is. In short, the second phrase of a period is hardly ever an answer to the first. How can one achieve true melody like that?

The *Scene in the Country*, which constitutes the third movement of the symphony, is characterized by such obscurity of thought, such unpleasing aimlessness, that it would perhaps be impossible to listen to it all the way through if one's boredom were not mitigated by some happy orchestral effects. In these passages, as everywhere else, there is a paucity of ideas, and the contrast of instrumental effects is the only recourse to which M. Berlioz always turns for rescue.

M. Berlioz's admirers have greatly puffed the *Execution March*, the fourth part of the symphony; its praises seem to me highly exaggerated. Doubtless there is more rhythm in this section than in the others, and there are a number of new effects. But there are innumerable digressions, and the harmony is all the worse for exhibiting a certain pretentiousness. In sum, though, it is the least faulty part of the *Fantastic Symphony*.

The fifth part, the *Dream of a Witches' Sabbath*, mingles the trivial, the grotesque, and the barbarous; it is a saturnalia of noise and not of music. The pen falls from my hand!

In a recently published article, M. Berlioz assures us that the day will come when the artist will no longer be harassed about the ideas his art embodies or the means he uses to express his thought.[7] That day has come, M. Berlioz! You may dare anything so long as nature has created you to be a musician, so long as you possess a feeling for beauty, so long as you have imagination; but, by the very token that you use such huge resources, don't hide behind your pretensions, and don't exhibit your impotence! In a word, if you possessed what you basically lack, if you had true imagination, you would be allowed everything, and today's critics would become your admirers. Until then, you may take it for granted that your restless posturing will be in vain: your present output will remain unworthy of consideration as works of art!

ROBERT SCHUMANN

A Symphony by Berlioz [†]

Robert Schumann (1810–56) had three musical lives: he was a pianist, a composer, and a critic. It is the last that concerns us here. As one of the founders of the *Neue Zeitschrift für Musik*, as its editor, and as a

7. A reference to *Premier Bal de l'Opéra*, in the *Gazette musicale de Paris*, Jan. 18, 1835, an article in which Berlioz expressed his confident hope for a day when public and critics "will allow the artist full and complete freedom to formulate his own modes of expression." [*Editor*]

† *Neue Zeitschrift für Musik*, July 3 and 31, August 4, 7, 11, and 14, 1835. Translation by the editor.

lively contributor to its pages, he affords us the satisfying spectacle of a great musician who was both quick to recognize talent in others and unfailingly generous toward it.

His analytical critique of Berlioz's *Fantastic Symphony* is his most extended essay and one of his most famous. In the issues of February 27 and March 3, 1835, the *Zeitschrift* had published a communication from Paris, "Hector Berlioz and his Compositions," by Heinrich Panofka (1807–87, at that time a well-known violinist, later to become a voice teacher). Panofka's glowing account, appearing hard on the heels of Fétis's sour notes in the *Revue musicale*, prompted Schumann to study the score for himself and to write his own rebuttal of Fétis. But in a model of critical fair play, he first published a translation of the Fétis article in the *Zeitschrift* (June 19 and 23), prefacing it with the following "Editor's Note":

> We have previously mentioned the critique in Mr. Fétis's journal, the *Revue musicale*; at that time we were not familiar with the symphony or with Berlioz's work in general. We thought that Heinrich Panofka's letters about the same symphony stood in such interesting contrast to the derogatory tone of M. Fétis's review that we straightway wrote to Paris for the symphony itself. It has been in our hands now for several weeks. We have gradually arrived at our own opinion; and it is by and large so strongly opposed to that of M. Fétis that we have decided to set before our readers a clear translation of his review. This we do partly to create a twofold occasion for bringing the gifted republican to German attention, partly to provide some of you with an opportunity of making the comparison for yourselves. Our own verdict will follow as soon as possible. Until then we urgently recommend that those who are interested in extraordinary things should try to get acquainted with the symphony itself.

Schumann's promised review appeared on July 3, and after a few weeks continued from July 31 through August 14. As thus printed, it consisted of two parts. The first, which was confined to the original installment, was a short, enthusiastic appreciation couched in highly poetic language. It was signed "Florestan," the pen name Schumann used when his writing expressed the impassioned, romantic side of his nature. Presumably the much longer analytical and critical section that followed (five installments) was meant to be by "Eusebius," the composer in his more reflective and judicial mood, but it is actually signed "R. Schumann."

In 1854, when Schumann published a collected edition of his essays, he omitted Part I entirely and made some excisions from Part II. This abridged version is the one most often reprinted. So far as I know, the present translation is the first complete one. Those passages omitted from the revised version are enclosed in brackets; the rare phrases added in revision are in double brackets. There are, in addition, a few differences in wording between the two editions. Where substantial, these have been noted; but some of them are too idiomatic to show up successfully in translation.

The essay is extensively annotated by references to Liszt's piano transcription. I have converted all of these to refer to the orchestral score. (Roman numerals indicate the movements; arabic numerals denote the measures.) At the same time I have tried to correct obvious misprints and to suggest alternatives for a few questionable readings; all such cases are fully annotated. Where convenient I have incorporated Schumann's footnotes into the text.

[1]

[Let us enter battle, not with a wild cry like our early German forefathers, but like the Spartans to the sound of joyful flutes. To be sure, the one to whom these lines are dedicated needs no shield-bearer; he will, it is to be hoped, contrary to the fate of the Homeric Hector, prove victorious in the end and drag as a prisoner behind him the downfallen Troy of outworn tradition. But if his art is a flaming sword, let this word be its protecting scabbard.

My first look at the symphony filled me with the strangest emotions. As a child I would often put music upside down on the stand, in order to enjoy the oddly interlaced patterns of notes (as later I came to enjoy the reflections of Venetian palaces inverted in the water). Right side up, this symphony resembled such inverted music. Then other scenes from the writer's earliest childhood came to mind, such as one midnight, everyone in the house already asleep, when he crept, dreaming with eyes fast shut, to his old piano (now demolished) and struck chords that made him weep profusely. When they told him about it in the morning, he remembered only a strange-sounding dream and many unusual things he had heard and seen; and he clearly discerned three mighty names, one in the South, one in the East, and the last in the West—Paganini, Chopin, and Berlioz.[1] The first two, with eagles' strength and swiftness, have achieved first rank; it was easy for them, since each of them united in his person the roles of playwright and actor. It will be more difficult for the orchestral virtuoso Berlioz, and he will have to fight harder, but perhaps he will win a more splendid wreath of victory. Let us try to hasten the moment of decision! The ages struggle on perpetually; let the future decide whether forward or backward, whether for good or ill. But categorically to predict the latter course as certain for our own time—no one has been able to do that to my satisfaction.

After having gone through the Berlioz symphony countless times, at first dumbfounded, then shocked, and at last struck with wonderment, I

1. A highly prophetic dream, at least with respect to Chopin and Berlioz, as a glance at their dates will show! [*Editor*]

shall try to make a quick sketch of it. I will depict the composer to you as I have come to know him, in his weaknesses and his virtues, in his vulgarity and his nobility, in his destructive anger and his love. For I know that what he has produced cannot be called a work of art, any more than Nature itself without human cultivation, or passion without the restraint of higher moral force.

If old Haydn cultivated character and talent, religion and art equally, if Mozart's ideal artistic nature developed independently of his natural sensuality, if other poetic spirits found their personal lives completely at odds with their artistic output (as, for example, the licentious poet Heidenreich,[2] who wrote the most mordant poem against concupiscence), then Berlioz belongs more to the Beethovenian type of those whose life history corresponds exactly to their artistic development, every changing impulse in the former being reflected in the progress of the latter. Like a Laocoön serpent, music clings to Berlioz's feet, and he can take no step without it; he rolls in the dust with it; it enjoys the sun with him; even if he would exorcise it, he would still have to do so to music; and if he should die, his spirit would perhaps dissolve into the music we so often hear hovering over the distant horizon at noon, the hour of Pan.

This man, so highly musical, barely nineteen years old,[3] of French blood, exuberant with energy, battling moreover with the future and perhaps in the throes of other violent passions—this man is seized for the first time by the god of love—not, however, that timid feeling that prefers to confide in the moon, but rather the gloomy fire one sees at night pouring forth from Etna. . . . And here he sees *her.* I imagine this feminine creature to be like the main theme of the whole symphony, pale, slender as a lily, veiled, quiet, almost cold—but my words make one sleepy, while its tones burn into one's very entrails. Read in the symphony itself how he rushes toward her, eager to surround her with his soul's embrace, and then recoils breathlessly from the coldness of the British woman; how he offers, with renewed humility, to lift the hem of her dress to his lips, and then stands proudly erect and *demands* her love,

---

2. Karl Heinrich Heidenreich (1764–1801), professor of philosophy at the University of Leipzig, who was forced to resign in 1798 for irregular conduct. [*Editor*]

3. Schumann is of course all wrong here. Later he speaks of Berlioz as an eighteen-year-old, but puts the first performance of the symphony in 1820, which would actually make him a seventeen-year-old! He may have been unsure of Berlioz's birth date; he certainly was misinformed about the date of the symphony. One possible explanation for his mistake has already been suggested; see pp. 29–30. [*Editor*]

since his love—for her—is so terrifying: read it again, for it is all written there in the first movement with drops of blood.

First love can well make a captain out of a coward, but "a heroine does great harm to a hero," as Jean Paul[4] has put it. Sooner or later, fiery young men whose love is unrequited throw Platonic spirituality overboard and make countless sacrifices at the altars of Epicureanism. But Berlioz is no Don Juan. With glassy eye he sits among dissolute companions; and every pop of a champagne bottle being broken open is answered by the snap of a string broken inside him! The well-known, beloved figure arises before him on every side—out of the very walls, as if to a feverish man—and lies oppressively upon his heart. He repulses her, and a whore, laughing loudly, throws herself on his lap and asks what is wrong with him.

Artistic Genius, here is where you come to the rescue of your darling, and well indeed does he understand the quivering smile on your lips! What music in the third movement! This intimacy, this remorse, this ardor! The image of Nature's sigh of relief after a storm is one that has often been adduced, but I can think of none lovelier or more fitting here. The world still shudders from Heaven's embrace and a thousand eyes brim over with dew, while the timorous flowers tell one another of the strange visitor who now and then still looks around and thunders.

Now, this is where one who wanted to earn the name of "Artist" would have stopped and celebrated the victory of Art over Life. But *she*, but *she*! Tasso was thus driven into the madhouse.[5] But in Berlioz the old destructive fury awakens redoubled, and he lays about him with real Titan's fists. And just as he, dazzled by the artistic illusion of possessing his beloved, warmly embraces the artificial figure, so too the music, loathsome and vulgar, wraps itself around his dreams and around his attempt at suicide. The bells toll, and skeletons play the organ for the wedding dance. . . . Here Genius, weeping, deserts him.

It seems to me, though, as if I sometimes heard even in this movement, very faintly indeed, sympathetic vibrations with that poem of Franz von Sonnenberg that sounds the keynote of the whole symphony:

> Du bist's—und bist das glühend ersehnte Herz,
> Durch stumme Mitternächte so heiß ersehnt

* * *

4. J. P. F. Richter (1763–1825), who wrote under the pseudonym of Jean Paul, was an important German romantic novelist and one of Schumann's favorite authors. [*Editor*]

5. It is true that the great Italian poet suffered from mental illness; but this was probably not caused by an unhappy love affair, as was at one time popularly supposed. [*Editor*]

Du bist's, die einst süßschauernd am Busen mir
In langen Tiefverstummen, in bebenden
    Gebrochnen Ach's verwirrt, mit holdem
        Jungfrauerröten ins Herz mir lispelt:
"Ich bin das Ach, das ewig die Brust dir eng
"Zusammenkrampft' and wieder zum Weltraum hob.

           * * *

"Dein erster Seufzer rief schon unwissend mich:
"In jeder wild auflodernden Andachtsglut
    "War ich's in dir, dem du die Hände
    "Faltetest. * * *

"In allem ich, wonach du im Leben nur
"Bei hoher Brust die Arm' auseinander warfst."

           * * *

Du warst, du bist das große Unnennbare,
Wonach in Götterstunden mein Herz sich hebt,
    Sich hebt, o wenn die ganze Menschheit
        An mich zu drücken ich wollustbebe.

           * * *

Einander fassen!—zweite Unsterblichkeit!
Des Wonneschauers aller Natur in mir!
    Des Augenblickes, Herkla, wenn wir
        Zitternd and stumm nun einander fassen![6]]

                [Florestan]

6. Franz von Sonnenberg (1779–1805) was a minor German poet best known for his epic poem, *Donatoa*, written in imitation of Klopstock. He committed suicide at the age of twenty-six. The above lines may be rendered:

    It is you!—you are the heart so ardently desired,
    So passionately desired through silent midnights;
    It is you who once lay sweetly shuddering on my breast,
    Confusing me now with long, deep silence,
    Now with broken, quivering "Ah's";
    And, with a maiden's sweet blush, you whispered to my heart:
    "I am the 'Ah' that ever tightly contracted your breast
    "And then expanded it into lofty space.
    "Your first sigh unknowingly summoned me:
    "In the wild flame of every passionate prayer
    "It was I within you to whom you folded your hands.
    "I am a part of everything in life
    "To which you, high of heart, extend your arms."
    You were, you are the great Ineffable,
    Toward which, in sacred hours, my heart aspires—
    Aspires, oh, when I tremble with desire
    To embrace all mankind.
    To hold each other! A second immortality—
    Of the thrill of delight all Nature feels within me,
    And of the moment, Herkla, when, trembling and mute,
    We hold each other!

    A perusal of these verses may explain why Schumann eventually excised this section. [*Editor*]

[II]

[I have read attentively both Florestan's words about the symphony and the symphony itself, I may say, down to the tiniest note. But it seems to me, although I am pretty much in general agreement with his initial judgement, that this psychological approach to the criticism of the work of a composer known only by name, about whom the most contradictory opinions are expressed, is insufficient, and that this critique, favorably disposed toward Berlioz, could easily become the object of all kinds of suspicious doubts excited by its failure to discuss the actual musical composition.

I now realize that it is the job of a more than merely poetical type to assign to this remarkable work its proper place in art history—it takes, that is, a man who is not only a philosophically trained musician but also one with an intimate knowledge of the history of the other arts, who has given thought to the significance of artistic phenomena and to their cross-connections, as well as to the meaning underlying their sequence. Nevertheless, one might well listen also to the word of a musician who pursues in his own creative work the aims of the younger generation and who defends, body and soul, its loftiness of purpose, but who, all the same, would not hesitate in open court to sentence his favorite to a beating—although he would perhaps gladly pardon him in private. Of course this time more laurels than cudgels will be needed.]

The manifold material that this symphony offers for consideration could so easily become entangled in the following discussion that I prefer to break my analysis into sections, even though any one of them may often depend on the others for clarification. I shall divide it according to the four points of view from which a musical work can be examined: *form* (of the whole, of each movement, of period, of phrase), the *compositional fabric* (harmony, melody, continuity, workmanship, style), the *specific idea* that the artist wanted to present, and the *spirit* that rules over form, material, and idea.

Form is the vessel of the spirit. Greater spaces require greater spirit to fill them. The word "symphony" has hitherto designated instrumental music of the greatest proportions.

We are wont to judge objects by the names they bear; we make certain demands of a "fantasy," others of a "sonata."

It is enough for second-class talents to master the received forms; those of the first rank are granted the right to enlarge them. Only the genius may range freely.

After Beethoven's Ninth Symphony, in external dimensions the greatest of all instrumental works we have, moderation and limit seemed to be exhausted. [The gigantic idea needed a giant's body; the god, a world to work on. But art has its boundaries. The Apollo Belvedere a few feet taller would be offensive. The later symphony composers realized this, and a few even fled back to the traditional forms of Haydn and Mozart.]

Here [also] should be mentioned: Ferdinand Ries, whose originality was such that only Beethoven's could overshadow it; Franz Schubert, the imaginative painter who dipped his brush equally into moonbeams and flaming sun, and who might have given us a tenth Muse after Beethoven's nine[7]; Spohr, whose gentle voice did not resound strongly enough in the great symphonic vault where he tried to speak; [Onslow, who, in spite of an undeniable talent for instrumentation, was not skillful enough at covering the bare bones of his four-part writing;] Kalliwoda, that happy harmonious being, whose later symphonies, laboriously built on deep foundations, failed to attain the heights of fancy of his first. Among recent composers we know and admire Maurer, Schneider, Moscheles, C. G. Müller, Hesse, Lachner, and Mendelssohn, whom we have taken pains to mention last.[8]

None of the above, who, except for Franz Schubert, are all living, dared make any substantial changes in the old forms, with the exception of isolated experiments like Spohr's latest symphony.[9] Mendelssohn, an artist important both for productive capacity and for intellectual insight, apparently realized that there was nothing more to be gained in this direction, and struck out on a new course, one which Beethoven, to be sure, had already traversed with his great *Leonora* Overture.[10] With his

7. A reference, of course, to Beethoven's nine symphonies. As Schumann added later in a footnote, "The Symphony in C had not yet appeared at that time." Moreover, the Unfinished Symphony was not generally known until after Schumann's death. [*Editor*]

8 Not an imposing list. Only Mendelssohn, Schubert, and to a lesser extent Ludwig (Louis) Spohr (1784–1859) have survived as composers. Johann Wenzel Kalliwoda (1801–66), Czech violinist and composer, is occasionally revived, while Ferdinand Ries (1784–1838) is best known for his biography of Beethoven. Ignaz Moscheles (1794–1870) is, of course, remembered as a great pianist, but hardly as a composer. George Onslow (1784–1853), despite his name, was French; he wrote a quintet describing his accidental injury, during a hunt, by a stray bullet. Ludwig Maurer (1789–1878), Friedrich Schneider (1786–1853), Christian Gottlieb Müller (1800–63), Adolph Hesse (1808–63), and Franz Lachner (1803–90), all German contemporaries of Schumann, are now only so many entries in a biographical dictionary. [*Editor*]

9. A program symphony, *Die Weihe der Töne* (The Consecration of Sound, 1832). [*Editor*]

10. Originally: ". . . struck out on a new course, although one might say that the path had been blazed to a certain extent by the first *Leonora* Overture." In 1835,

concert overtures, in which the idea of the symphony is confined within a smaller orbit, he won crown and scepter over all other instrumental composers of the day. It was to be feared that from now on the name "symphony" would belong only to history.

Abroad, composers were silent. Cherubini spent long years working on a symphony, but is said to have confessed his incapacity—perhaps too soon and too modestly. All the others in France and Italy were writing operas.

Meanwhile, in an obscure corner of the northern French seacoast a young medical student contemplates something new. Four movements are too few for him; he uses five, like the acts of a play. At first I took Berlioz's symphony to be written in emulation of Beethoven's Ninth (on other grounds than the five-movement form; this would be no reason at all, for the Ninth has four movements). But the *Fantastic* was first performed at the Paris Conservatory in 1820, before Beethoven's appeared, so that there can be no question of imitation. Now courage, and on to the symphony itself![11]

If we look at the five movements in relation to one another, we find that they comply with the traditional succession, except for the last two, which, however, as two scenes of a dream, seem to form a single whole. The first movement begins with a slow section, which is followed by an Allegro; the second takes the place of the Scherzo; the third, that of the central Adagio; the two last constitute the final Allegro. In tonality as well they are closely related: the introductory Largo is in C minor, the Allegro in C major, the Scherzo in A major, the Adagio in F major, the last two movements in G minor and C major. So far so good. Now if I could also succeed in giving the reader, whom I should like to accompany upstairs and down through this wonderful building, a picture of its individual rooms! [We have often read of those old Scottish castles, described for us with such fidelity by English writers, and in our mind's eye have enjoyed the randomly placed windows and the boldly jutting towers. Look at our symphony in the same way: follow me now through its fantastic network of corridors.]

The slow introduction to the first Allegro differs but little from

the Overtures No. 1 and No. 2 were not yet generally known, so that Schumann is referring to No. 3, the "great *Leonora* Overture." By the time the essay was revised, all the overtures had been published; hence the "great" was no longer the "first." [*Editor*]

11. This paragraph not only repeats the error of date already pointed out (see p. 223, n. 3), but adds a new one: "the northern French seacoast." [*Editor*]

those of other symphonies (I am speaking here of form only), except by virtue of a well-defined organization that will strike anyone who tries various rearrangements of its larger sections. There are actually two variations on a theme, with free interludes between. The main theme extends to I, m. 16; an interlude to m. 27; the first variation to m. 41; an interlude to m. 50; the second variation, over the held bass note, to m. 58 (at least, I find in the horn solo the melodic figures of the theme, although only vaguely suggested).[12] Now a striving toward the Allegro; introductory chords; we pass from the vestibule into an inner room: Allegro.

Anyone who now insists upon staying to examine individual details will be left behind and will lose his way. Look quickly over the whole passage from the opening theme to the *a tempo con fuoco* at m. 111. Three ideas have so far been stated in close connection: the first (which Berlioz calls *la double idée fixe* for reasons to be explained later) goes to m. 86; the second (borrowed from the introduction) to m. 103; and the third continues until the *a tempo* at m. 111.[13]

The following section should be taken as a unit up to m. 150—but don't overlook the passage, *un peu retenu*, at mm. 119–25. At m. 150 we reach an especially well-lighted area (the true second theme) from which we can look back over the ground we have already covered. The exposition now closes and is repeated.

From here on the periods seem to be trying to achieve a clearer succession but are forced by the thrust of the music now to expand, now to contract: thus they run from the beginning of the development to the passage in parallel six-threes (m. 200), and thence to the staccato chord of m. 230, which brings matters to a standstill.

Now a horn in the far distance. Something very familiar rings through up to m. 280. Here the trail becomes harder to follow and more mysterious. Two ideas, of four and nine measures respectively; passages of two measures each; freestanding arches and paths that change direction.[14] The second theme, subjected to ever closer stretto, eventually appears in its full glory, ending at m. 331. The third phrase of the first

12. Whether or not one accepts Schumann's suggestion that this section represents a second variation, mm. 49–59 would constitute a more natural division, and one more in accordance with Schumann's own description ("over the held bass note"). I suspect that either a miscount or a misprint is involved here. [*Editor*]

13. Actually Berlioz's *idée fixe* seems to comprise all three of Schumann's "ideas." [*Editor*]

14. Schumann does not locate these, but the measures to which he refers are clearly mm. 280–83, 284–92, 293–94, 295–96, 297–98, 299–312. [*Editor*]

theme[15] now descends to ever lower levels; then darkness.

Little by little the shadowy outlines assume living form, up to mm. 371–72; the initial pattern of the main theme undergoes the most distorted fragmentation until m. 411. Now the entire first theme, in terrifying splendor, up to the *animez*, m. 441; and now completely fantastic shapes, which remind us of familiar ones only once, and then as if smashed to pieces. All vanishes.

Berlioz [[, who studied medicine in his youth,]] probably never dissected the head of a good-looking murderer more reluctantly than I have dissected his first movement. And have I been of any help to my readers with my post mortem? I had three aims in performing it: first, to prove to those totally unfamiliar with the symphony that the illumination of the music available to them from an analytical critique is indeed slight; second, to indicate a few high points to those who have looked over the symphony superficially and have perhaps set it aside, being unable to find their way about in it; last, to demonstrate to those who know the work but fail to appreciate it that, despite its apparent formlessness, a symmetrically ordered pattern governs its larger proportions—not to mention the inner consistency of the movement. But the unfamiliarity of this new form, of this new mode of expression, is bound to lead to unfortunate misunderstanding. Most listeners fasten too strongly onto details at first or second hearing. The same thing happens when we read a difficult handwriting: if, while deciphering it, we pause over each individual word, we need disproportionately more time than if we first scan the whole passage for its meaning and purpose. Besides, as I have already suggested, nothing arouses disagreement and opposition so quickly as a new form bearing an old name. For example, if someone decided to call a piece in $\frac{5}{4}$ time a march, or twelve successive short movements a symphony, he would certainly prejudice his own case ahead of time—although one should always try to find out how matters really stand. Thus the more unusual and ingenious a work appears to be, the more careful one should be in judging it. Isn't our experience with Beethoven an example?—Beethoven, whose works, especially the last ones, were at first considered incomprehensible, as much for their original structures and forms, which revealed such inexhaustible invention, as for their spiritual content, which of course no one could deny!

If we now try to comprehend the entire first Allegro as a wide-arching whole, without being disturbed by small, though to be sure,

15. Actually not this phrase, but the related idea from mm. 119–25, as Schumann himself indicates later. [*Editor*]

often sharply projecting, corners, this form becomes clear:

```
                        First theme
                         (G major)

              Middle sections       Middle sections
              with a second         with a second
                  theme                 theme

         First theme                          First theme
          (C major) ........................... (C major)

      Beginning                                         Close
      (C major)¹⁶...(G major, E minor)...(E minor, G major)......(C major)
```

This we can compare with the traditional model:

```
                        Middle section
                          (A minor)

                   Second theme              First theme
     First theme    (G major)... (Development of ...(C major)   Second theme
     (C major).....................both themes)....................(C major)
```

We could not guess what advantages of unity or variety the second form is supposed to have over the first; but let us say in passing that we wish we, too, possessed such an enormous imagination and could just let go!

Something still remains to be said about the structure of the individual phrases. The music of our day can offer no example in which meter and rhythm are more freely set to work in symmetrical and asymmetrical combinations than in this one. Hardly ever does consequent correspond to antecedent, or answer to question. This is so characteristic of Berlioz, so well in accord with his southern nature and so strange to us northerners, that our discomfort at first encounter and our complaints of obscurity are both pardonable and explicable. But the daring by which all this has been achieved, in such a way that nothing can be added or subtracted without depriving the musical idea of its pointed urgency and its power —of this one can be convinced only by seeing and hearing for oneself.

[Whereas the Goethe-Mozart period is rightly called the loftiest epoch of art, a time when the imagination bore the fetters of rhythm as lightly as crowns of celestial flowers,] it seems that in the present instance music is trying to return to its origins, when it was not yet bound by the law of the downbeat, and to achieve on its own a prose style or a higher poetic articulation (as in Greek choruses, or the language of the Bible, or

16. Actually C minor, as Schumann has already pointed out. I wonder also whether the "G major" of the recapitulated second theme is not a misprint for "C major." See the amended diagram on p. 252. [*Editor*]

Jean Paul's prose). We refrain from developing this idea further, but in closing this paragraph we shall remind you of what that childlike, poetic spirit Ernst Wagner[17] prophesied, [in his well-known ingenuous manner. Somewhere he says: "The nightingale's song, too, embodies movement; one might call it the rhythm of melody. But there is no stability of tempo, whether fast or slow; no subordination of all individual freedoms and movements to one superior law; hence no fundamental rhythm. Meter must once have afforded a very salutary sensation, one which we often enjoy even today. In fugues, sometimes in the case of dissonances, and always with difficult contrapuntal clashes, meter, more than anything else, calms us, since it is itself a calm and perpetually unchanging measure of time. On the other hand, in slow, sweet, or languishing melodies the meter keeps us going, driving us irresistibly forward from measure to measure until the end. But, in truth, from another point of view meter does so much harm that, under its present sway, our music cannot aspire to the rank of a fine art (or, as others put it, to independent consciousness); for though music might well be capable of presenting something like a finely conceived idea, it is manifestly restricted. If we are to hear a convincing form, music must act as freely as poetry on our conceptual capacities. Meter, however, does not allow this so long as it applies only to the measure of duration but not to that of syllables and even beyond, failing at any event to encompass large open structures corresponding to poetic stanzas. Prosody enjoys great freedom in music, but duration depends on strict laws. We know of no complete movement in so-called *ad libitum*; the performer has really only the freedom to start and to stop, for between beginning and end reigns the tyrannical meter alone (which is actually a human invention, which one has to be taught), under whose orders performer and listener must remain in conspicuous servitude. All attempts to withstand meter only make its dictatorial pressure more perceptible.] He who is destined to conceal and render imperceptible the tyranny of the bar in music will, at least apparently, set this art *free*; he who then bestows upon it the gift of *consciousness* will empower it to present finely conceived ideas, and from this moment on it will be the *first* of all the fine arts." [Could this moment be at hand with the symphony of Berlioz?]

As we have said, it would take us too far afield and would be of no avail to dismember the other movements of the symphony as we have the first. The second turns in various directions like the dance it is meant to

17. Ernst Wagner (1769–1812), German novelist and playwright, a friend of Jean Paul. [*Editor*]

portray; the third, perhaps the loveliest, soars skyward and descends like a rainbow; the last two lack a central point and push incessantly toward the end. In spite of all superficial formlessness, we cannot fail to appreciate the intellectual coherence of the work, and one might remember here that verdict, wry though it is, on Jean Paul, whom someone called a bad logician and a great philosopher.

So far we have been dealing with the garment; now we must look at the cloth it is made of, at the *compositional fabric*.

At the outset I must point out that I have only a piano transcription as a basis for my judgment, albeit one that indicates the most important details of instrumentation. Even if this were not the case, everything seems to me conceived and worked out so completely in orchestral terms, with each instrument so exactly placed and exploited, so to speak, with regard for its basic sonorous quality, that a good musician could prepare a passable score from the arrangement—naturally excepting the new combinations and orchestral effects on which Berlioz is known to lavish his attention. [But more of this later.]

If ever a judgement appeared to me unjust, it is the one summarily given by M. Fétis's words: *"Je vis qu'il manquait d'idées mélodiques et harmoniques."*[18] He might deny Berlioz everything, as indeed he has: imagination, invention, originality—but richness of harmony and melody? [There is no way to answer that.] I have no intention of arguing against this otherwise brilliant and witty review, for I find in it no personal animus or injustice, but rather, to be frank, blindness: the lack of an organ for the perception of this kind of music. But my reader is not expected to believe anything he cannot find out for himself! Although individual extracts torn from context are often misleading, nevertheless I shall try by this means to demonstrate the individuality of the whole work.

With respect to the *harmonic* value of our symphony, one certainly recognizes here the awkwardness of the eighteen-year-old composer who, paying little attention to left or right, makes straight for his goal. If Berlioz wants to get from G to D♭, for example, he proceeds without ceremony (Ex. 1).[19] One may well shake one's head over such doings! But musically intelligent people who heard the symphony in Paris affirmed

18. "I saw that he lacked melodic and harmonic ideas." This paragraph originally began: "If anything has ever seemed inexplicable to me, it is the summary judgement M. Fétis has given in the words:." [*Editor*]

19. At this point, when Schumann revised the essay he added a reference to "p. 16" (I, m. 331), which makes no sense. I take it to be a misprint for "p. 61" (IV, m. 130), an even better example than his own illustration, which is an alternation of two chords, not of two keys. See n. 22. [*Editor*]

Ex. 1.

that the passage could not be otherwise. Indeed, someone dropped the noteworthy remark about Berlioz's music: *"Que cela est fort beau, quoique ce ne soit pas de la musique."*[20] [To this a French critic d'Ortigue made reply: *"S'il en est ainsi, M. Berlioz est sans contredit le génie le plus étonnant qui ait paru sur la terre, car il s'en suit forcement qu'il a inventé un art nouveau, un art inconnu, et pourtant un bel art."*[21]] Although such talk is to no particular purpose, it is still worth repeating.

Besides, I find that such irregularities occur only exceptionally.[22] I would even assert that his harmony, despite the varied combinations he derives from restricted material, is marked by a certain simplicity, in any case by a solidity and conciseness, such as we find, though of course in a more developed form, in Beethoven.

Does he perhaps depart too far from the main key? Look at just the introduction: first section (up to I, m. 27), clear C minor; thereupon he faithfully repeats the intervals of this first idea in Eb major (m. 28); then he remains for a long period over Ab (m. 46) and modulates easily into C major. From the sketch of the Allegro that I have given above, one can see how that movement is constructed from the simplest relations of C major, G major, and E minor. And so it goes throughout. The entire second movement is penetrated by the sharp sound of bright A major; the third by the idyllic F major and its related C and Bb majors; the fourth, by G minor with Bb and Eb majors. Only in the last movement, despite the prevailing tonality of C, does disorderly confusion reign, which is only fitting for an infernal wedding.

At the same time one does often come up against harmonies that are

---

20. "It's very beautiful, although it isn't music." [*Editor*]

21. "If that is so, then M. Berlioz is without doubt the most astonishing genius who has ever appeared on the face of the earth, for it necessarily follows that he has invented an art that is new and unknown, yet beautiful." Joseph-Louis d'Ortigue (1802–66), French musicologist and critic, was a close friend of Berlioz. [*Editor*]

22. Compare, however, IV, mm. 129–30.

flat and ordinary;[23] or faulty, at least forbidden by the old rules (though some of these sound splendid) [24]; or unclear and vague[25]; or ugly in sound, tortured, twisted.[26] May the time never arrive that would sanction such passages as beautiful! [It would be as unwelcome as an age that declared hunchbacks and madmen to be Apollos and Kants.]

But Berlioz's case is a special one: just try to change or to improve anything, as it would be child's play for any skilled harmonist to do, and see how dull [and insipid] everything becomes by comparison! For beneath the first eruptions of a strong, youthful temperament lies a wholly individual, indestructible force; no matter how crudely it may express itself, its effect is all the more powerful the less one attempts through criticism, to bring it into line with accepted artistic standards. It would be fruitless to try to give it professional polish, or to force it to remain within bounds, until it has learned for itself to manage its own resources more thoughtfully and to discover rules and limits of its own.

23. I, mm. 21–22, 43–45, 64–71, 488–91; II, mm. 302–19.

24. Right at the outset in I, m. 1, the B (probably a misprint). [Schumann's guess is wrong; the doubled leading-tone appears in every score and is clearly intentional. In a touch of subtle orchestral coloring, which Schumann could not have deduced from the piano score, the lower doublings enter here as if they are only gradually becoming audible. At the same time, the G-B-C of the bassoon may refer to the exploitation of these three notes later in the Largo (I, m. 3, in first and second violins, mm. 9–10 in first violins and cellos) and in the *idée fixe* itself (I, 72–79) .— *Editor*] I, mm. 24–26, 108–09, 115–19, 142–45, 441–51; II, mm. 348–51, 365–66; III, mm. 146–47; IV, mm. 76, 154–59; V, mm. 307–09 and all that follows, mm. 388–89 and all that follows, mm. 408–12, 464–66, 483–84. I repeat that I am judging only by the piano transcription: much of this may seem different in the score. [Quite so. Many of the parallel fifths and octaves that Schumann found are due to the piano arrangement.—*Editor*]

25. I, m. 441; perhaps the harmonies are as follows:

6   7   6   6♯   6♭   6♮   6   6♯

3♯ -   3 —   3♭ —   3—

D♯   E   F   F♯   *etc.*

[For a musically notated version of this analysis, see Ex. 8, p. 260. Schumann's reference here to "p. 20, m. 3" must be a misprint, since that turns out to be I, m. 436. What is clearly meant is p. 20, system 2, m. 3, which begins the passage Schumann has analyzed.—*Editor*] IV, mm. 158–59; V, m. 11, probably a joke of Liszt's, who may have been trying to imitate the dying away of the cymbals. V, mm. 317–19, 348 and what follows, 491–93, and others. [Schumann's guess about the cymbals, which actually do not occur at the passage cited, was wrong; the harmony is as Liszt transcribed it.—*Editor*]

26. I, mm. 21–22, 36, 115–19, 371 and quite a bit beyond; II, mm. 160–61; V, mm. 387–94, 491–93, and others. [(The reference to V, m. 387–94, was puzzlingly obscured when the essay was reprinted, for Schumann's "p. 82" became "p. 28.") For an interesting discussion of Schumann's reasons for questioning Berlioz's harmony, see Leon B. Plantinga, *Schumann as Critic*, New Haven, 1967, pp. 239–44.—*Editor*]

Berlioz does not want to be taken for polite and elegant: what he hates,
he seizes violently by the hair; what he loves, he nearly crushes in his
ardor—give or take a few inches, for one has to be indulgent with a fiery
youth whom one can't measure by ordinary yardsticks!

But we should also seek out the many passages of sensitive and beautiful originality which balance those that are rough and bizarre. Such is
the [pure and noble] harmonic construction of the entire first cantilena
(from I, m. 3 on) and of its repetition in Eb (m. 28). The Ab held for
fourteen measures in the bass should be most effective (m. 46), as well as
the pedal in the inner voices (m. 168). The ponderously ascending and
descending chromatic sixth chords (m. 200) are meaningless in themselves but must sound uncommonly impressive in context. From the transcription, it is impossible to judge those passages where imitations
between bass (or tenor) and soprano produce ugly octaves and false relations (m. 371); if the octaves are well concealed, such passages must cut
to the quick.[27]

The harmonic basis of the second movement is, with a few exceptions, simpler and less profound. The third can compare in purely harmonic value with any [[other symphonic]] masterwork: here every tone
is alive. The fourth is consistently engrossing and is in the tersest, pithiest
style. The fifth rants and rages in excessive confusion; except for a few
novel passages[28] it is unlovely, shrill, and disagreeable.

Although Berlioz may tend to neglect individual parts and to sacri-
fice them for the sake of the whole, he is nevertheless a master of the
ingeniously conceived and finely wrought detail. He does not, however,
squeeze the last drop out of his themes, spoiling our pleasure in a good
idea, as others so often do, by boring thematic development. Instead, he
gives hints that he could work things out in stricter fashion if he wanted
to, in suitable context—sketches in Beethoven's epigrammatic manner.
His loveliest ideas are almost always stated only once, as if in passing
(Ex. 2).[29]

27. See, for example, oboe and viola in m. 374, and oboe and cello in m. 375,
for octaves; cello and oboe in mm. 373–74 and viola and flute in mm. 384–85, for
false relations. For pianistic reasons the transcription does not always preserve Berlioz's voice leading; sometimes Berlioz's bass becomes Liszt's tenor, etc. [*Editor*]

28. V, from m. 269 on; from m. 329 on, where Eb is sustained in an inner voice
for twenty-nine measures; the dominant pedal beginning at m. 362; the passage beginning at m. 386, where I tried in vain to get rid of the unpleasant fifths at mm.
388–89. [Schumann was misled by the transcription here. The "dominant pedal"
(which really begins at m. 363) is Liszt's version of a long bass-drum roll. The
"unpleasant fifths," too, are the result of Liszt's rearrangement of parts and his
octave doublings.—*Editor*]

29. I, mm. 24, 280–92, 360–68, 429–43; III, mm. 49–64. [The fourth citation would
read better, "429–41."—*Editor*]

Ex. 2.

* When the essay was reprinted, this indication was erroneously applied to the next example. [*Editor*]

The principal motif of the symphony (Ex. 3) is neither significant in itself nor amenable to contrapuntal treatment, but it improves more and more on acquaintance through its later appearances. It has already

Ex. 3.

become more interesting at the beginning of the development, and continues in this direction (Ex. 2; I, m. 362) until it struggles through shrieking chords into C major (m. 412). In the second movement the composer constructs a trio from it, note by note in a new rhythm and with new harmonies (II, m. 120). Toward the end it returns once again, but feebly and haltingly (m. 302). In the third movement it appears as a recitative interrupted by the orchestra (III, m. 90): here it undertakes to express the most fearful passion, up to the shrill A♭, where it seems to collapse in a swoon. Later (mm. 150, 160) it reappears, gentle and

calm, guided by the main theme of the movement. In the *Marche du
supplice* it tries to speak out again, only to be cut off by the *coup fatal*
(IV, m. 164). In the dream it is played on the vulgar-sounding clarinets
in C and E♭ (V, mm. 21, 40), shriveled, dishonored, and besmirched.
Berlioz did that deliberately.

The second theme of the first movement seems to stem directly from
the first (I, m. 150); they are so closely intergrafted that it is hardly possible to discern their dividing point until finally the new idea breaks free
(Ex. 4), shortly to reappear, although almost imperceptibly, in a lower
voice (mm. 163, 194). Later the composer takes it up once more and out-

Ex. 4.

Ex. 5.

lines it most ingeniously (Ex. 5); this example shows his method of development at its clearest. Equally sensitive is his later completion of an idea that one might assume he had totally forgotten (mm. 119, 331).

The motifs in the second movement are less artfully intertwined, but the appearance of the theme in the lower voices produces a first-rate effect[30]; his development of a single measure of this theme is elegant (II, m. 106).

The monotony of the main idea of the third movement is relieved by charming variations on its return (III, mm. 20, 69, 131); Beethoven could hardly have given it more careful treatment. The whole movement is full of ingenious interconnections. Thus at one point Berlioz quits low C by a downward leap of a major seventh[31]; later he makes good use of this insignificant motif (Ex. 6).

Ex. 6.

In the fourth movement the counterpoint between the chief theme (Ex. 7) and its countersubjects is masterfully worked out; also worthy of

Ex. 7.

note is the careful management of the various transpositions to E♭ major (Ex. 8) and back to G minor (Ex. 9).[32]

In the last movement Berlioz introduces the *Dies irae* first in whole

30. II, mm. 176, 338. The effect is intensified in the transcription, where the theme is made the true bass. Here and elsewhere I have translated Schumann's "bass" as "lower voice" to conform with the score. [*Editor*]

31. In the cello, III, mm. 111–12. This leap is even more obvious in the piano version, where the C is not doubled in the lower octave. [*Editor*]

32. IV, mm. 33, 49, 82, 114, 123, and then inverted in m. 131. [Again I have corrected a misprint. Schumann's second citation is "p. 57, m. 12," which refers to part of the second theme (m. 69). I have assumed that he meant p. 56, m. 12, which gives m. 49.—*Editor*]

Ex. 8.

Ex. 9.

notes, then in halves, then in eighths[33]; it is accompanied by bell strokes
on tonic and dominant in a regular pattern. The following double fugue

33. V, mm. 126, 147, and 157. [Schumann is not accurate here: the theme begins
in m. 127 and appears in dotted halves, dotted quarters, then in quarters and
eighths.—*Editor*]

Ex. 10.

(Ex. 10), which Berlioz modestly calls only a fugato,[34] is certainly not by Bach but is nevertheless clearly constructed according to the rules. The *Dies irae* and the *Ronde du sabbat* are well interwoven (Ex. 11).

Ex. 11.

But the theme of the latter is not long enough, and the new accompaniment is as free and easy as can be, consisting of ascending and descending scales in thirds.[35] The last five pages are all topsy-turvy, as was often mentioned before; here the *Dies irae* begins once again, this time pianissimo.[36] Without a score, one can only call the last pages poor.

If M. Fétis maintains that even Berlioz's warmest friends would not dare to defend him as a melodist, then I belong among Berlioz's enemies; but one must not think in this connection of melodies of the Italian type, which one knows [by heart] even before they have begun.

34. This term appears in the transcription, not in the score. [*Editor*]
35. The thirds are Liszt's contribution, for the sake of pianistic brilliance. [*Editor*]
36. IV, m. 486. [The *Dies irae* is not actually pianissimo here, although the accompaniment fluctuates between *pp* and *ff*. (When the essay was reprinted, this footnote and n. 32 were transposed; I have restored the correct correlation.) —*Editor*]

It is true that the chief melody of the whole symphony, which I have mentioned several times, is undistinguished; and Berlioz praises it almost too much when he attributes to it in the program a "noble and shy character" (*un certain caractère passionné, mais noble et timide*). But we must remember that his intention here was not to present a great thought, but rather a persistent, tormenting idea of the kind that one often cannot get out of one's head for days at a time; and he could not have succeeded better in depicting something monotonous and maddening.

In the same review we are told that the chief melody of the second movement is common and trivial; but surely Berlioz here wants nothing more or less than to take us to the ballroom (somewhat like Beethoven in the last movement of the Seventh Symphony). [That's the way it is: whenever a great man gets familiar and walks the earth with common folk, they exclaim at his condescension. But they don't see his head, which is still in the clouds above.] It is the same with the opening melody of the third movement (Ex. 12), which M. Fétis, I believe, calls

Ex. 12.*

> * The notation of the transcription here follows an earlier version as found in the manuscript. [*Editor*]

gloomy and tasteless. But just wander about the Alps and other shepherds' haunts and listen to the shawms and alphorns; that's exactly the way they sound.

Indeed, all the melodies of the symphony are just as characteristic and natural; and in certain episodes they strip off their peculiarities and reveal a more universal and loftier beauty. What fault, for example, can be found with the cantilena that opens the introduction? Perhaps its range exceeds a ninth? Or isn't it melancholy enough? What about the sorrowful oboe melody in one of the preceding examples?[37] Does it make some improper leaps? But who wants to point his finger at every detail!

If you must find fault with Berlioz about something, it should be about his neglect of inner voices; but in his defense stands a peculiarity that I have observed in few other composers. I mean the fact that his

37. Obviously Ex. 2. [*Editor*]

melodies are distinguished by such intensity of almost every individual tone that, like many old folksongs, they often defy ordinary harmonization and would lose sonority if subjected to it. Berlioz therefore generally harmonizes them with a pedal or with simple dominant and subdominant chords.[38] To be sure, you must not listen to his melodies with the ear alone; if they are not to pass you by uncomprehended, you must be able to follow them by singing inwardly—and not in an undertone, but with full[, unceasing] intensity. Then they will assume a meaning whose implications will seem more profound at every repetition.

For the sake of completeness, let us now add a few remarks about the symphony as an *orchestral composition* and about *Liszt's piano transcription*.

A born virtuoso of the orchestra, Berlioz naturally makes terrifying demands, both on individuals and on the ensemble—more than Beethoven does, more than all others do. But it is not greater mechanical dexterity that he requires of the instrumentalists; what he wants is sympathy, study, love. The individual player must withdraw in favor of the group, which in turn must submit to the will of its leaders. Nothing can be accomplished in only three or four rehearsals; in this respect one may think of the symphony as occupying the same place in orchestral music as the Chopin Concerto[39] occupies in piano music, although I should not like to push the comparison further.

Even Berlioz's opponent, M. Fétis, does full justice to his instinct for instrumentation. I have already mentioned that one can figure out the solo instruments from the bare piano score. Nevertheless it would be difficult for even the liveliest imagination to form an adequate idea of the various combinations, contrasts, and striking effects. To be sure, Berlioz shrinks from nothing that can be called tone, sound, noise, or clangor; thus he uses muffled drums, harps, muted horns,[40] English horn, finally even bells. Florestan has said that he greatly hopes that one day Berlioz will have all his musicians whistle together—although he might as well write rests, since the players, overcome by laughter, would be hard put to purse their lips. And when Florestan reads scores in the future,

---

38. For the former, see, e.g. I, m. 412, and III, m. 131. For the latter, the chief melody of the *Ball*, where the fundamental harmonies are those of A, D, E, and A. [Schumann then refers to "p. 47, m. 1 in the *March*," but this is an error, for it merely repeats the second of these citations. Perhaps he intended the second theme, IV, m. 62.—*Editor*]

39. Only the E minor was published at this time. [*Editor*]

40. On muffled drums and muted horns, see the Textual Note, pp. 200-01 and 211. [*Editor*]

he will be looking for singing nightingales and occasional thunderstorms. Enough of this—one must now hear the work. Only in this way shall we learn whether the composer's demands are justified, and whether they lead to a proportionate gain in pleasure. It is uncertain whether Berlioz can accomplish anything using more economical means. Let's be content with what he has given us.

Franz Liszt's piano transcription deserves extended discussion. We shall save that for the future, along with a few observations on the symphonic treatment of the piano[; today we shall be brief]. Liszt has applied so much industry and enthusiasm [and genius] that the result, like an original work summarizing his profound studies, must be considered as a complete manual of instruction in the art of playing the piano from score. This kind of interpretive art, so different from the filigree work of the virtuoso—the various kinds of touch that it demands, the effective use of the pedal, the clear interlacing of individual voices, the grasp of the texture as a single block of sound; in short, the thorough knowledge of the medium and of the many secrets that the piano still hides—this can only be the work of a master and genius of performance such as Liszt above all others is well known to be. But in such a case the piano arrangement need not fear being heard side by side with an orchestral performance; indeed, Liszt recently played it publicly in Paris as the introduction to a later symphony by Berlioz (the *Mélologue,* a sequel to the *Fantastic*). [This piano arrangement is certainly unique and must be recommended as such to those who wish to learn the rare art of symphonic performance; we feel it is our duty to voice here our warmest recognition of the credit Liszt so well deserves.

A word must nevertheless be said in passing about the careless *orthography* of the transcription. Carping criticism looks for anything to use as a weapon against unusual phenomena, and that is the case here. It's hard to attack a lion with needles, but you can at least disconcert him.]

Let us look back for a moment at the path we have so far traversed. According to our original outline we were going to discuss form, compositional fabric, idea, and spirit, in separate sections. First, we saw that the form of the whole differs but little from the traditional, that the various movements have adopted patterns that are mostly new, and that the relationships of phrase and period are completely distinctive by virtue of their unusual proportions. Under compositional fabric, we called attention to the harmonic style, to the ingenious working of details, connections, and contrasts, to the originality of the melodies, as well as to the instrumentation and the piano transcription. We shall now close with a few words on idea and spirit.

Berlioz himself has written down in a program what he wants us to think about when hearing his symphony. Here it is in brief:

The composer's intention was to depict in music certain passages from the life of an artist. It seems necessary for the outline of an instrumental drama to be explained verbally before the performance. One should consider the following program as analogous to the dialogue leading into the musical numbers of an opera.

First movement: "Dreams, Sufferings" (*Rêveries, passions*). The composer supposes that a young musician, afflicted with that moral disease that a well-known writer calls *le vague des passions*, sees for the first time a woman who embodies all the charms of the ideal being he has imagined in his dreams. Through an odd whim of chance, whenever the beloved image appears before his mind's eye it is linked with a musical thought whose character, passionate but at the same time noble and shy, he finds similar to the one he attributes to his beloved. This melody and this image pursue him incessantly like a double *idée fixe*. Dreamy melancholy, which, interrupted by only a few tentative notes of joy, climbs to heights of amorous frenzy; sadness; jealousy; inner fervor; tears—all these aspects of first love constitute the subject-matter of the first movement.

Second movement: "A Ball." In the midst of the tumult of a festival the artist stands in rapt contemplation of the beauties of nature[41]; but everywhere, in town, in the country, the beloved image appears before him and disturbs his peace of mind.

Third movement: "Scene in the Country." One evening he hears two shepherds piping a *ranz des vaches* in dialogue; this duet, the scenery, the quiet rustling of the leaves, a glimmer of hope of requited love—all concur in affording his heart an unaccustomed calm and in giving his thoughts a friendlier direction. He reflects on the possibility that his loneliness may soon be over—but what if she were deceiving him! This shift between hope and sorrow, light and darkness, is expressed by the Adagio. At the end one of the shepherds again takes up the *ranz des vaches*; the other no longer replies. Thunder in the distance—loneliness—deep silence.

Fourth movement: "The March to the Scaffold" (*Marche du supplice*). The artist is convinced that his love is not returned, and poisons himself with opium. The narcotic, too weak to kill him, plunges him into a sleep filled with the most horrible visions. He dreams that he has killed her and that, sentenced to death, he is witnessing his own execu-

41. Schumann must have misread the program here. One will also note other slight differences from the standard version. [*Editor*]

tion. The procession begins; a march, now sombre and fierce, now brilliant and solemn, accompanies it; muffled sound of steps, rough clamor of the crowd. At the end of the march, like a last thought of the loved one, appears the *idée fixe*, but only half of it, interrupted by the blow of the ax.

Fifth movement: "Dream of a Witches' Sabbath." He sees himself in the midst of frightful grotesques, witches, monsters of every kind, come together for his funeral. Wails, howls, laughter, lamentation. The beloved melody sounds once again, but as a vulgar, sordid dance theme: it is *she* who comes. A roar of joy at her arrival. Devilish orgies. Funeral knell. A parody of the *Dies irae.*

Thus the program. All Germany is happy to let him keep it: such signposts always have something unworthy and charlatan-like about them! In any event the five titles would have been enough; word of mouth would have served to hand down the more circumstantial account, which would certainly arouse interest because of the personality of the composer who lived through the events of the symphony himself. In a word, the German, with his delicacy of feeling and his aversion to personal revelation, dislikes having his thoughts so rudely directed; he was already offended that Beethoven should not trust him to divine the sense of the *Pastoral Symphony* without assistance. Men experience a certain timidity before the genius's workshop: they prefer to know nothing about the origins, tools, and secrets of creation, just as Nature herself reveals a certain sensitivity when she covers over her roots with earth. So let the artist lock himself up with his woes; we should experience too many horrors if we could witness the birth of every work of art!

But Berlioz was writing primarily for his French compatriots, who are not greatly impressed by refinements of modesty. I can imagine them, leaflet in hand, reading and applauding their countryman who has depicted it all so well; the music by itself does not interest them.

Whether a listener unfamiliar with the composer's intent would find that the music suggested pictures similar to those he wished to draw, I cannot tell, since I read the program before hearing the music. Once the eye has been led to a given point, the ear no longer judges independently. But if you ask whether music can really do what Berlioz demands of it in his symphony, then try to associate with it different or contrasting images.

At first the program spoiled my own enjoyment, my freedom of imagination. But as it receded more and more into the background and my own fancy began to work, I found not only that it was all indeed there, but what is more, that it was almost always embodied in warm, living sound.

Many listeners worry too much in general about the difficult question of how far instrumental music should go in the representation of thoughts and events. One is certainly mistaken if one believes that composers take up pen and paper just with the paltry idea of expressing, or describing, or painting this or that. But one should not underestimate the importance of chance influences and impressions from outside. Along with the musical imagination there is often an idea unconsciously at work; along with the ear, the eye; and this ever-active organ, in the midst of sounds and tones, holds fast to certain outlines that can solidify and take clear shape as the music develops. The greater the number of musical analogues suggested by the thoughts or pictures to be produced in tone, the more poetic or plastic in expression the composition will be; and the more imaginative or keen the musician's powers of perception, the more uplifting or gripping his work will be. Why shouldn't thoughts of immortality occur to a Beethoven during his flights of musical fancy? Why shouldn't the memory of a great fallen hero inspire him to a composition? Why shouldn't the memory of a bygone golden age inspire another?[42] Or should we be ungrateful to Shakespeare for evoking a work worthy of himself from the breast of a young tone-poet? Ungrateful to Nature, by denying that we have borrowed some of her beauty and nobility in our own works? Italy, the Alps, a seascape, a spring dawn—has music told us nothing of these?

Even smaller, more specific pictures can lend such a charmingly exact character to music that we are surprised at its powers of delineation. Thus a composer told me that once while writing down a composition he was constantly obsessed by the image of a butterfly floating away on a leaf in a brook; this had imparted to his little piece as much tenderness and simplicity as the actual scene could have revealed. Schubert was a special master of this delicate genre painting, and in this connection I cannot resist recounting an experience of my own. Once while playing a Schubert march, I asked the friend playing with me whether unusual images weren't taking shape before his eyes. He answered: "Really, I thought I was in Seville, but over a hundred years ago, in the midst of Dons and Doñas strolling up and down, wearing trains, pointed shoes, poniards, etc." Strangely enough, our two visions coincided even to the

42. Originally: "Why shouldn't the memory of a heavenly night enjoyed by ardent young lovers inspire another?" The reference. as the next sentence shows, is to *A Midsummer Night's Dream*, and to Mendelssohn's Overture, written in 1826. [*Editor*]

exact city. I hope the [gentle] reader will allow me this trivial example!

Whether the program of Berlioz's symphony contains many poetic elements, we leave as an open question. What remains as really important is whether the music, without text and explanation, has intrinsic value, and especially whether it is imbued with spirit. I believe I have already demonstrated something about the first point; as for Berlioz's spirit, it is undeniable, even where his defects are obvious.

If one insisted on setting oneself against the mind of the times, against a *Zeitgeist* that tolerates a burlesque of the *Dies irae*, one would have to repeat what has been written and said for years against such men as Byron, Heine, Victor Hugo, and Grabbe.[43] At certain moments in eternity Poetry may put on the mask of irony to veil her sorrowful face; perhaps a [[genius's]] friendly hand will one day remove it, [and we shall find that her unrestrained tears have been changed into pearls.

A little while ago Odilon Barrot made a remark that speaks directly to the heart of today's youth: *"Dans notre époque, je ne sais qui s'est imaginé que tout ce qui est dans la nature est beau, qu'il y a une certaine poésie dans le crime."*[44] In plain words, "Beware, you young people, of being seduced into misdeeds by Nature and Passion. Follow Nature's call, speak your mind as sincerely as you can, according to your affections and your indignations. But preserve your innocence, which alone renders Nature worthy of love: it may err, but never sins; it gives delight, but never satiety."]

We could go on for a long time discussing the rights and wrongs here, but this is enough for now!

If these lines should help induce Berlioz once and for all to moderate his eccentric tendencies, if they should gain recognition for his symphony, not as an artist's masterpiece but as a work unique in its originality; if, finally, they should excite more vigorous activity among German artists, to whom Berlioz has extended a firm hand in fellowship against untalented mediocrity, then their publication will have achieved its purpose.[45]

43. Christian Dietrich Grabbe (1801–36), German poet and playwright, whose subjects were often grotesquely fantastic. [*Editor*]

44. "These days the idea has got around that everything in nature is beautiful, that there is a certain poetry in crime." Barrot (1791–1873) was a French lawyer and politician. [*Editor*]

45. The last sentence originally ran: "If this essay should help persuade Berlioz that the extravagance of his spirit should no longer depend on the excuse that it is the product of genius; if it should gain recognition for his symphony, not as an artist's masterpiece but as a work unique in its intellectual vigor and originality; if, finally, it should excite more vigorous activity among young Germans, to whom Berlioz has extended a firm hand in fellowship against untalented mediocrity, then in truth it will have achieved its purpose." [*Editor*]

EDWARD T. CONE

Schumann Amplified: An Analysis

Schumann's strategy is a familiar one: in order to induce his readers to accept a new form, he tries to convince them that it is not really so new after all. Thus he correlates the movements of the *Fantastic Symphony* with those of the classical model by pointing out the resemblance of the first three to the sonata allegro, dance movement or scherzo, and slow movement, respectively, and then by combining the last two into one superfinale. Berlioz himself may have had the same kind of justification in mind when, in the manuscript, he labeled the last two movements as the First and Second Parts of the Vision. But in the end he decided, quite properly, that these movements are just as independent as the other three, and he frankly admitted that he had composed a five-movement symphony. (And why not? Beethoven had written one long ago.)

This realization may have contributed to the decision to place the *Ball* before the *Scene in the Country*; now the long central Adagio is flanked by two shorter dance movements (for a march is, after all, a kind of dance). The reversal may also have been motivated by the composer's desire to make more cogent certain tonal connections that we shall examine as we go along. Still another probable reason was the revised ending of the Adagio, with its lonely shepherd, bereft of his partner, piping in the face of a menacing storm. The kettledrums used here to imitate the sound of thunder play an even more threatening role at the beginning of (and indeed throughout) the March. The connection is both musically and psychologically apt.

The key relationships of the movements form a clear pattern: I–VI–IV–V–I in C. But two points here deserve more than the passing comment Schumann bestowed: VI is represented by A major rather than A minor, and V by G minor rather than G major. In spite of the innovations of Beethoven and Schubert, such indirect tonal relationships were still exceptional. Perhaps that is why Berlioz softened the striking harmonic contrast in an oddly symmetrical manner: the second move-

ment *begins* in A minor (coming from C major) and the fourth movement *ends* in G major (leading back to C) .

FIRST MOVEMENT: Rêveries. Passions

Schumann is, of course, right when, pursuing his tactics, he relates
the *Rêveries. Passions* to the classical sonata form with slow introduction.
But his zeal leads him to look too eagerly for parallelisms and symme-
tries, and as a result he finds some that are not there. The introduction
certainly contains a theme and variation, separated by an episode; but to
find a second variation in what follows is to ascribe to the section a
kind of neatness it does not have. Schumann himself was diffident about
this, admitting that the thematic substance is "only vaguely suggested"
(*nur anklingend*) by the horn at I, mm. 50–59.

An analysis of this "variation" that does more justice to the com-
plexity of the introduction would see it as a huge elaboration of a basic
VI (A♭) in C minor. The motif A♭-G is prominent in the theme from
the outset: see the first violins at mm. 3 and 5, and the cellos at m. 3.
Expanded harmonically, the motif underlies mm. 7–10, a phrase that
begins on VI and ends on a V that, by virtue of being a ninth chord,
combines A♭ and G simultaneously! The same motif in the bass acts as a
transition (mm. 15–17) to the tonic major of the interlude.

When the theme returns in its varied form (harmonized at first in
E♭ major, III) , the measures corresponding to mm. 15–16 are expanded
to fill mm. 40–48, the VI now elaborated to include the Neapolitan (II♭
or N): essentially VI–IV–N–V–VI. Now comes the passage in question, which Schumann called a second variation, but which we can now
see is part of a huge VI–V–I—an expansion of the cadence of mm.
16–18. Here Berlioz uses a characteristic device: chords constantly shift-
ing over a bass note that harmonizes with all of them. With great sub-
tlety A♭ is enharmonically changed to G♯, which in turn acts as a leading
tone to another form of VI, A♮. And now, at last, the goal is clear: the C
major of the Allegro, which is greeted with three definitive cadences.
Here is the Largo in outline:

A	1–2	Introductory V–I in C minor; winds alone.
	3–16	Theme in muted strings: Phrase 1, 8 measures, I–V; Phrase 2, incomplete, 6 measures, III–VI, completed by:
	16–18	Transitional cadence: VI (or IV⁶)–V–I (major) .
B	18–24	Interlude in C major, returning to C minor. Unmuted strings and winds.
	24–27	Transitional, moving to V of III.

A
28–48	Variation on theme, stated now by unmuted strings with elaborate wind accompaniment. The harmonies are partially reversed: Phrase 1, 8 measures, III–V; Phrase 2, incomplete but expanded to 13 measures, I–VI (see above for details), leading to:
49–59	Expansion over A♭, completed by:
60–63	First cadence in C major,
63–64	Second cadence in C major,
64–72	Third cadence in C major.

Thus in the most general terms we have two statements of a theme, each working by way of VI–V to C major (mm. 3–18, 28–63), separated by an interlude and followed by clinching cadences; in other words, an ABA. But rounded off though the form seems to be, there is no finality: the tempo quickens, and the last cadence overlaps by elision with the entrance of the first theme of the Allegro.

Schumann is on the right track when he describes the Allegro as what might be called an arched sonata form, i.e. one with first and second themes reversed in the recapitulation. His diagram, though, in its search for symmetry, leaves out much that is important for a thorough understanding of the movement. The same is true, for that matter, of the corresponding diagram of the traditional form, which reduces the development section to the expansion of a single key area—here, by way of example, indicated as the relative minor. (For an approximation of Schumann's outline, see the first movement of Mozart's Piano Sonata in C, K. 309.)

A more accurate and complete diagram of the Berlioz movement would show a form symmetrical enough, with the keystone of the arch the same as Schumann's: the striking return of the first theme in G, after the general pause. The symmetry is violated only by the two bracketed sections, which are lacking in Schumann's diagram (see p. 252).

He likewise omits reference to transitional and episodic material. Particularly important here is what I call the Cadential Phrase, the passage at mm. 119–25. It is very similar to the last phrase of Theme A (mm. 103–11), and at one point Schumann even confuses the two (see p. 229, n. 15). Both of them are initiated by the descending seventh, a persistent motif in this movement. Sometimes the seventh appears as a direct leap (as in m. 104), sometimes partially filled in (as in the Cadential Phrase), sometimes completely filled in by thirds (as in the bass, mm. 64–70). Perhaps these descending thirds are the true source of this entire complex of ideas; they are first heard between alternating woodwinds and pizzicato strings in the approach to the Allegro (m. 63).

Theme A

Episode--------Transition

Theme B :‖ [Dev. of Th.A-Th.B]

Dev. and
----Recap. of
Th.B

Transition with
Cadential Phrase----------------------------------Recap. and Dev. [Dev. of Th.A]
of Cad. Phr.

Recap. of
Th.A

‖ Theme A--

Introduction--Coda

m.72	111	150	168	193	200	234	280	313	331	360	412	477
C minor	C major											
I	I	I-V of V -	V(-III-V) V - I	I - V of II II - V V - VI	III-VI-I I - V of II	III-VI-I I - V of II	- II-V-I	I

Ex. 1.

Schumann duly notes the derivation of the second period of Theme A (m. 86 ff.) from the introduction. But one should be aware, too, that the figure F♯-G-F♮-E of mm. 83–86, as well as the characteristic leading-tone cadence of mm. 78–79, is also derived from the introduction. And, finally, the contrast between the minor and major sixth degrees (A♭ and A♮), so striking in the theme, was used (in the bass) to turn the end of the introduction toward C major. Example 1 clarifies these relationships.

Schumann's divisions of Theme A into three main sections is clear enough. Ignoring the short upbeats we have:

72–86   Section 1, a period of two parallel phrases, 8 and 7 measures. This is the kind of asymmetry that upset Fétis so much. It would be very easy to make the second phrase exactly parallel to the first (see Ex. 2) —but to do so is to understand how right Berlioz was.

87–103   Section 2, a model with three sequences, of which the last is expanded; hence 4, 4, 4, and 4½ measures.

103½–11   Section 3, a cadence of 8 measures.

Ex. 2.

The importance throughout the symphony of this *idée fixe*, not to speak of its subsequent fame or notoriety, is such as to make it worthwhile spending a little time on its melodic and harmonic structure. Example 3 is a sketch of its linear shape. (The bass in this example will be explained shortly.)

The melody is stated by a unison of flute and violins. The other strings interject a peculiar accompaniment figure, consisting always of two detached eighth notes. This rhythm was prepared at the appearance of the new tempo at m. 64, and it will be found playing an important role throughout the rest of the movement. The original accompaniment, as a look at the manuscript will show, included a string tremolo as well. This may have been conventional in sound, but it made the underlying harmony easier to grasp than it now is. For example, it stated what we are evidently meant to assume in the final version: a dominant ostinato from mm. 78 through 85. Thus the apparent tonic in m. 84, so startling and even disturbing on the heels of the immediately preceding F♯, stands for a I$^6_4$ and is therefore a preparation for a dominant, no longer stated

Ex. 3.

Top line of Ex. 3 contracted for easy reading

but understood, in m. 85. Yet the identical accompaniment figure in the next measure represents a true tonic! (See Ex. 4.) The deliberate ambi-

Ex. 4.

1, 83

* This appears to be correct, but there is a bad smudge on the manuscript here.

guity of the harmony can be somewhat mitigated in performance, but it was obviously Berlioz's intention that it should be dissipated only later—partially at the recurrence of the theme in G, and completely at the recapitulation in the tonic. For purposes of comparison, the original cello line, which was the lowest continuous part and hence what I take to be the true bass, is shown in Example 3 (up to the cadence, where the original version departs considerably from the final one).

The tutti that sets in at the conclusion of Theme A exploits familiar motifs: the E-F-E from the first phrase of the theme (mm. 113–15), and the chain of thirds, now both descending and ascending (mm. 115–18), accompanied by a familiar rhythm in the basses. It it interrupted by the Cadential Phrase, against which we hear an augmentation of the accom-

Ex. 5.

paniment rhythm. (The manuscript shows this augmentation to be a later revision; originally the eighths were retained here.) At m. 133 a definite turn toward F minor (IV) initiates a transition leading through A♭ (VI) to D (II). The appearance of Theme B in the dominant completes the progression as N-V-I in G. Example 5 shows the origin of the principal ideas of this section.

The second theme, which enters at m. 150, is, as Schumann says, so closely intertwined with the first that the new idea seems to have a hard time breaking away. There are three phrases, each introduced by the principal motif of Theme A:

> 150–54 2 measures of A (flute and clarinet in octaves), leading to 3 measures of B (strings). VI–I in G (Schumann's E minor and G major) but no cadence. (Notice that the accompanying rhythm of A still persists!)
>
> 154–60 2 measures of A (as before), 5 measures of B (strings plus woodwinds), VI–I, with a perfect cadence. This overlaps with:
>
> 160–66 2 measures of A (flute, clarinets and oboes), 5 measures of B, with a new counterpoint (strings plus winds). This time there is a perfect cadence with no overlap. (The first ending adds a seventh to G, converting it into a clear V.)

The first phase of the development leads to the general pause at m. 230. It can be divided into three sections: rising sequences on the first idea of Theme A, progressively truncated; a recapitulation of Theme B in the tonic; and an episode based on chromatically ascending and descending chords of the sixth.

> 168–92 Expansion of V. A 4-measure model derived from mm. 72–75 initiates a chromatically rising sequence in the bass. The third and fourth statements are reduced to 2½ measures each; from there on a single measure suffices until the climax is reached on a reiterated V². Against this the woodwinds have been developing a counterfigure that can perhaps best be heard as a retrograde of the main idea (see Ex. 6).

Ex. 6.

I, 73, transposed:

I, 171

> 193–200 This appearance of the second theme, first in winds and then in strings, in two overlapping phrases of 4 and 5 measures, coming to a full cadence on I, may seem surprising here. But the tonic is not dwelt on; its rhythmic articulation is

immediately vitiated by the onset of the chromatic sixths. Moreover, it enters as a sixth (first inversion) and leaves as a sixth—the first of the episode. So the root position of the cadence is only an accent of detail. Finally, the tonic occurs surrounded by a dominant area, within which it functions as a subdominant. The overall harmonic motion may be heard thus:

m.	168	189	193	199–200	225	230	234	240
G:	I	V^2 of IV	IV^6	(V–I of IV)	V of V	V^6_5 of V	V	I

200–30 The rising and falling sixths are articulated by an ascending sequence in the woodwinds. Its model is the falling half step of m. 171.

Now we have the first return of Theme A, a complete statement in the dominant (mm. 241–80). It is preceded by a remarkable introduction. First, the A of the chord preceding the three-measure rest is answered by the long-held D of the horn. This interval is taken up in diminution by the violins; then, in further diminution, it is transposed to D-G. Thus the entrance of the theme on D-G is completely prepared—but this is not all. The rising D-G of the violins is answered by a falling D-G in cellos and basses, in a return to the rhythm and contour of the accompaniment of the theme in the exposition. What was not clear then is made clear now: the origin of that motif was to be found in the first two notes of the theme itself!

The melody is scored this time in double octaves: flute, clarinet, and bassoon; later the oboe is added. (Compare the unison presentation of its exposition, and the motif in single octaves that introduced Theme B). The harmonic clarification afforded by this statement has already been mentioned. (Notice, for example, the unambiguous V^7 of mm. 253–54.) But the final word on this subject is reserved for the statement yet to come.

Overlapping with the conclusion of the theme, a new developmental phase begins with the descending chromatic cello line in m. 277. Above it, statements of the half-step motif lead to a new idea that can be shown to be the progeny of Theme B (Ex. 7). After a threefold cadence (again on G), rising thirds lead to a climax preparing a contrapuntal development of Theme B (see Schumann's Ex. 5, p. 238). Stated in closer and closer stretto, this theme finally achieves a definitively cadential statement in the tonic (mm. 324–31). This time the key of G, in spite of its persistence, has been broken up by the contrapuntal passage, with its

Ex. 7.

emphasis on E and A. These harmonies, related equally to G (VI and II) and to C (III and VI), create an ambiguous area that is resolved in favor of C by the vigorous I–II–V–I hammered home in the bass. And at this point, as if to clinch matters, the cadential theme returns, over a tonic pedal in the timpani, for its own recapitulation. It is stated four times in all, each time slightly differently:

331–39　In C major, divided between woodwinds and, after a measure's pause, violins—9 measures in all.

340–46　In C major, violins, 7 measures, overlapping with:

346–53　Moving from C major to C minor, in cellos, 8 measures.

354–60　Moving from C minor to A major (! V of II), in cellos and basses, 7 measures. Note here the familiar play on the contrast of A♭ and A♮.

Just as the return of Theme A in the dominant was preceded by a chromatic episode, so now its climactic tonic statement is prepared by a long and highly chromatic development in which its opening motif is the subject of a dialogue between cellos and violas. Meanwhile, a new, widely ranging melody is developed by the oboe—a melody that sounds so spontaneous and free that it is hard to believe that it was a later addition to the otherwise complete texture; but such the manuscript attests that it was. (Perhaps this is why the passage does abound in the parallel octaves and false relations that Schumann noted.) From its inception in m. 360 to its triumphant arrival on the dominant in mm. 408–11, this section is harmonically almost as vague as the episode of mm. 200–30; for, like the earlier passage, it is largely based on rising and falling chromatic sixth chords, although they now proceed much more slowly. But there is no question as to the goal when we emerge from the chromatics: the dominant seventh is completely convincing, and the tonic recapitulation of Theme A (m. 412) is thoroughly satisfying.

This statement is the occasion for the first appearance of the trumpets and cornets: this is the first—and only—full tutti in the whole movement, which thus stands as a reproach to those who think of Berlioz as a noisemaker. The harmony is finally made explicit—e.g. the $I\,{}^6_4$-V^7-I of mm. 418–19. Even the phrase structure is regularized; up to the point where there is a departure from the normal cadence, we have:

412–15   4 measures corresponding to 8 of the original.
416–19   4 measures corresponding to 7.
420–25   Three 2-measure groups corresponding to three 4-measure groups.
426–29   4 measures corresponding to 4½.
430–33   4 measures corresponding to 8. But at this point we are diverging from the theme. A new countermelody (flutes) is heard above the final phrase (oboes), which never arrives at its tonic. Instead, we have:
434–37   4 measures repeating the preceding, but beginning a modulation.
438–41   4 measures continuing the modulation, arriving on V^6 of III.

What follows might now be considered the beginning of the coda, except for the fact that the recapitulation has not yet achieved its cadence. I therefore prefer to think of it as an interruption, the true coda appearing after the tonic of m. 477. The divisions are clear:

441–52   The rapidly moving harmonic passage that somewhat puzzled Schumann. Example 8, which translates his analysis (p. 235, n. 25) into musical notation and continues it to the half cadence on V, shows the relation of this progression to the familiar chromatic sixths.

Ex. 8.

452–63 Imitative passage based on Theme A, returning to V of III.

463–77 Repetition and extension of mm. 441–52, coming to a full cadence on I.

477–93 A development of the preceding idea in diminution (and retrograde-inversion?—see Ex. 9), leading to a cadence similar to the one that introduced the Allegro (mm. 63–65). This was the original coda, for the first version of the movement ended here.

Ex. 9.

493–504 The descending fourth E-B, from the first phrase of Theme A, is filled in chromatically by the oboe, over a string figure derived from the first four notes of the same theme. The last three measures prolong the dominant.

505–27 Final statement of the opening of Theme A, disappearing into inner voices so that it takes part in a long plagal cadence. But the theme can still be traced in the alternation of minor and major subdominants, as Example 10 shows.

Ex. 10.

SECOND MOVEMENT: *Un Bal*

Like Schumann, I have felt it necessary to go through the first movement in great detail. Its form is original and complex; its phrase structure is unusual; and its first theme, as the *idée fixe* which is to pervade the rest of the symphony, deserves close attention. The other movements are easier to deal with—particularly the second, which, as Schumann saw, is basically a waltz in which the *idée fixe*, suitably transformed, is heard as a free trio. Thus:

Intro.	A (with trans. to →)	B (with trans. to →)	A	Coda
m. 1	39	121	176	257

The introduction is reminiscent of at least two passages in the preceding movement. Its opening, I–VI in A minor, comes directly from I, m. 60; and the following progression is very similar to the one outlined in Example 8. In the present case the goal is I $^6_4$-V⁷, which is reached at mm. 30–32. A cadence on the tonic major and three measures of waltz accompaniment then prepare for the main theme, which enters with an upbeat in m. 38. Here, too, are connections with the past. The appearance of the "bright A major" (Schumann) recalls a striking modulation from the preceding movement (I, mm. 354–60); the contour of the theme, as it approaches its cadence (mm. 49–54), suggests a derivation from the subdivided descending seventh of the cadence at I, mm. 64–72 (see Ex. 11).

Ex. 11.

This section can be subdivided as a song form:

39–54   *a*: Violin I accompanied by strings alone; a double period of four 4-measure phrases ending with a full cadence on I.

55–93   *b*: Here the harps, which the introduction had already suggested as a significant feature of the orchestration, begin to assume importance. A 6-measure phrase, stated and repeated, remains in the tonic. A transitional scale in the woodwinds leads to two 9-measure groups (mm. 69–77, 78–86) which succeed in tonicizing V. But the second phrase is immediately extended by the addition of a seventh, and returns to the tonic by way of a cadence that skeletonizes that of the original theme (Ex. 11).

94–120   *a:* The return is regular until the last phrase, which initiates an imitative extension (commended by Schumann) leading through a deceptive cadence, V–VI♮, to the entrance of the new idea in a key suggested as early as the fifth measure of the movement. But the relationship of dominant to minor submediant is much older than that: it harks back to the opening Largo, and to the *idée fixe* itself. The contrast between this F♮ and the F♯ so prominent in the melody of Section A also recalls the A♭-A♮ relationship of the first movement.

Here, of course, we encounter the complete *idée fixe*, repeated almost note for note, but transformed into a waltz. Played by the woodwinds, it is accompanied by the strings, which, after reminding us of the rhythm of the original accompaniment from the preceding movement, settle down to reminiscences of the waltz theme and its own accompaniment. (This combination was a very late afterthought of the composer. See Textual Note, pp. 202-04.) The cadence of the *idée fixe*, stated by the strings in F♮ (VI♮), is immediately repeated by the strings in B♭ (N). This initiates a transition to V (mm. 163–75) that prepares for the return of Section A.

This time accompaniment and orchestration are enhanced, and the theme itself is extended:

176–91   *a:* 16 measures as before.
192–232 *b:* Now 2 measures longer than before. The difference occurs in the expansion of the cadence returning to *a*, and in the measure of silence preceding the tonic.
233–56 *a:* Now 24 measures, owing to a varied repetition of the second pair of phrases. For the first time the melody is given to the woodwinds.

The coda is long and comprises several sections:

257–72 Two 8-measure phrases, the first over a tonic pedal, the second moving to a V–I cadence.
273–88 A varied repetition of the foregoing.
288–302 Extended cadence.
302–19 The tempo slackens slightly for a reminiscence of the *idée fixe*

in its waltz version. The clarinet states it in D, so that the sustained A of the flute and the horn sounds like a temporary V. But, at the end of the second phrase, a new version of an old cadence restores the proper tonic (see Ex. 11).

320–37 Return of the original key and the original tempo, in a cadence that refers once more to VIᴴ–V.

338–68 A final 8-measure version of the waltz theme, stated twice, and rising through the strings. Its motif then serves for a fourfold repetition of answering tonics and dominants, leading to the final cadence.

The striking use of the harps in this movement has already been mentioned. One other detail of orchestration should not be overlooked. Originally it must have been Berlioz's plan to banish all brass but the horns from this movement and the next. At some point—perhaps for some specific performance or for some virtuoso player—he added a solo cornet part to the waltz.[1] It is too bad that it is not more often heard, since it is highly ingenious. Note how he first uses the instrument to point up important progressions: the arrival at V and its resolution at the end of the introduction (mm. 30–36); the development leading to the deceptive cadence (mm. 106–115); the return to the first section (mm. 171–75). From here on the cornet takes an increasingly active role; it even adds a new rhythmic counterpoint to the last phrase of the coda.

THIRD MOVEMENT: *Scène aux champs*

Superficially, the form of the third movement is similar to that of the second. Like the A major of the waltz, the new key, F, recalls an important modulation of its predecessor. Both movements consist of introduction, ABA, coda; in both, the central contrasting section is based on the *idée fixe*, and this theme returns during the coda of each. But in the Adagio these sections function in quite a different way. The introduction does not merely prepare the key and set the stage for the appearance of the main theme; it develops its own self-sufficient idea. Since the same idea returns at the end, the two sections constitute a frame that sets off the bulk of the movement, an ABA with its own coda. In large outline:

	Intro.	A (with trans. to →)	B (with trans. to →)	A	Internal Coda	External Coda
m.	1	20	87	117	150	175

1. See David Cairns, "Berlioz, the Cornet, and the *Symphonie Fantastique*," in *Berlioz Society Bulletin*, XLVII (1964), 2–6.

The 20-measure introduction (the last measure overlaps with the next section), with its antiphonal dialogue between English horn and oboe, constitutes an effective little tone poem in its own right; but its important connections with what has been heard and with what is to come should not be overlooked. The harmony, when it enters, is based on C-Db-C, a reference to the minor that is corrected in the C-D♮-C of the melody at mm. 18–19. But what is this if not still another reference, in transposed form, to the Ab and G so prominent in the Largo, and to the correction of G-Ab-G to G-A♮-G in the course of the *idée fixe*? The same motivic germ serves as a counterpoint to the first theme proper of the present movement: see the clarinet and horn at mm. 38–42.

Section A combines elements of a sonata-exposition with those of a set of variations:

20–33 a_1: The theme is stated by the unison of violins and flute that originally presented the *idée fixe*. There is, in fact, a vague similarity here to that idea, suggested by the rising stepwise sequence and by the very bare accompaniment, faintly reminiscent of the rhythm associated with the earlier theme. The melody is not completed, for its 14th measure is elided with:

33–48 a_2: A varied repetition, mostly in parallel thirds and sixths, proceeding to a perfect tonic cadence in its 16th measure.

48–64   *b*: First a 5-measure phrase on contrasting material, remaining in I; then an extended version of the same, appearing to be a 6-measure phrase moving to IV. But a diminished seventh instead of the expected IV leads, through a passage based on a characteristic dotted rhythm, to a cadence on III, 5 measures later.

65–68   A short transition, heralding a new accompaniment, leads to:

69–78 a_3: Dominant version of the theme, now in cellos and violas, accompanied by a new figure in the strings, plus the dotted-rhythm motif in the winds. The theme is interrupted in its 10th measure.

79–87   Motifs from *b* return to make a transition to a cadence on IV.

In the new key, Bb, a recitative-like melody in the bassoons and lower strings, bearing certain clear points of resemblance to the *idée fixe* (the opening motif and the Gb-F), introduces the return of that theme in the flute and oboe. Each phrase of the theme is prepared by a progressively shortened passage of recitative; but when "the shrill Ab" is reached, the recitative, getting out of hand, prevents the completion of the theme. The Ab is eventually interpreted as part of a diminished seventh leading to V of F; now, through the C-Db motif, strikingly assigned to the cellos in the descending seventh noted by Schumann, a cadence, familiar from the waltz (see Ex. 11), leads back to the return of Theme A in the tonic. The recapitulation unfolds thus:

117–31 a_4: Varied version in the pizzicato strings, with countermelodies in the winds. (How could Schumann have overlooked this one? Yet he leaves it out of his list of variations.) The cadence is altered so as to effect a modulation to V.

131–50 a_5: The theme is stated in unadorned form in Violin II and in a new figuration in Violin I. The winds now have a sustained counterpoint against it, emphasizing once more (but in reverse order) the contrast of A♮-G and A♭-G (mm. 136–38). The theme receives its greatest extension (20 measures) in order to return convincingly to the tonic.

The "internal coda" that now follows may be divided into four phases:

150–54   Two imitative figures: one in the winds, derived from the *idée fixe*, against one in the strings, from Theme A.

155–60   The development of the descending seventh that delighted Schumann. He derived it from the cellos in mm. 111–12, but I prefer to hear it as a reference to the last phrase of the *idée fixe*, with its descending sevenths leading, as here, to a tonic cadence. (See Schumann's Ex. 6, p. 239. But he should have continued the bassoon part through the next two measures, thereby completing another seventh.)

160–63   Last reminiscences of the *idée fixe*.

164–74   An extended cadence based on the motif of mm. 60–63.

Here the movement may once have ended, although we do not know the exact nature of Berlioz's revisions at this point. But the history of the program indicates that the following "external coda" was an addition to the original. The return of the English horn melody, almost complete but without the answering oboe, the menacing timpani chords that settle on F minor in simultaneous opposition to the major of the theme, the echo of the last phrase to produce a cadence—these produce one of the most telling passages in the symphony, and are the result of the composer's happiest afterthoughts.

FOURTH MOVEMENT: *Marche au supplice*

Berlioz, as we know, at one time paired the two last movements as parts of the vision. From one point of view at least, they are to be distinguished from the rest of the symphony: by their use of full brass and percussion. Trombones, ophicleides (today, tubas), bass drum, and other members of the battery now make their appearance; the trumpets and cornets return for the first time since the opening movement (except for the solo cornet added to the waltz) .

The March appears at first glance to be in sonata form. The double bar and repeat suggest:

Introduction	Exposition	Development	Recapitulation	Coda
m. 1	17	78	123	164

The first two sections are regular enough:

Introduction (mm. 1–17)

1–17   What is extraordinary here is the orchestral sound: the four-part chords for pizzicato basses, the stopped horns, the thirds in the timpani. The harmony offers no problems until the cadence, V^2–$I\,{}^5_3$ in G minor, which is highly irregular and typically Berlioz. He knew that the B♭ on the timpani would sound like a resolution of the C in the double basses.

Theme A (mm. 17–61)

17–24   Phrase of 8 measures, I–V, melody in lower strings, unaccompanied except for the cadence.

25–32   8 measures, modulating I–VI, melody now with counterpoint in the bassoons.

33–40   8 measures, VI–III (V of VI) , melody in violins with counterpoint in lower strings. The timpani triplets of the introduction have returned.

41–49   9 measures, VI returning to I, continuing the previous orchestration. But the 9th measure is elided with the next phrase, so that the general 8-measure periodicity is observed. Note, too, the harmonic parallelism of the four phrases, which may be indicated:

$$\text{I - VI} \mid \text{VI - I.}$$
$$\underbrace{\text{I - V - I}} \qquad \underbrace{\text{I - V - I}}$$

49–61   8 measures, I–I. The theme in the lower strings is played against its own inversion in the upper strings plus a new counterpoint in the bassoons. The last two measures are repeated twice again, and the final tonic is extended for a measure. But meanwhile the timpani and ophicleide have been preparing the turn to III by reiterating B♭. A rising scale leads to:

Theme B (mm. 62–77) , a double period initiated by a syncopated motif from the introduction.

62–65   A phrase of 4 measures, remaining on I of the new key.

66–69   4 measures, moving IV–V. The rising third of the theme is now heard in trombone and ophicleide, mm. 66–67.

70–73   4 measures, like the first.

74–77   4 measures, amplifying IV by its own IV, and by IV of IV of IV (D♭, m. 75) ! But the last is only a passing harmony (though it will prove important later on) , and the direction of the phrase is to a cadence, IV–V–I.

So far so good. (Though it is not clear how seriously one should take the direction to repeat the exposition. How could this be made convincing in performance? Some conductors take the repeat as referring only to the second theme, although the original parts indicate that one is expected to return to the first measure.) But now the development behaves very strangely:

78–81   Two statements of a modulation, B♭: I = G minor: III–V. For the first time, the strings take up the typical timpani rhythm.

82–88   Theme A in the tonic, broken up into a kind of *Klangfarbenmelodie* of pizzicato strings, arco, and winds. The phrase is not finished but modulates back to III.

89–104   An orchestrally amplified version of Theme B, complete.

105–08   A corresponding repetition of mm. 78–81.

109–14   A shortened form of mm. 82–88, remaining in the tonic.

114–23   Sequential treatment of the first motif of Theme A, over a rising scale that eventually achieves the tonic over a firm V–I cadence.

This definitive and climactic arrival certainly sounds like the beginning of a true recapitulation:

123–30   8-measure return of the opening phrase of Theme A, in full orchestra, ending with a surprising turn to C♯–D♭.

131–40   10-measure phrase beginning as an inversion of Theme A on D♭. But the phrase moves into sequences: D♭, A♭, E♭, B♭— thus revealing the origin of the distant harmony in the elaborated subdominant of Theme B (m. 75). From B♭, III, it is of course easy to make the return to I.

Let us look back for a moment. What is particularly odd is the way a huge repeated section (X) straddles the double bar marking the end of the exposition:

X			X		
Th. B :‖	Mod.	Phrase from Th. A	Th. B	Mod.	Phrase from Th. A
16 mm.	4 mm.	7 mm.	16 mm.	4 mm.	5 mm.

The result is an ambiguity of form. If we forget the sonata-form terminology and ignore the double bar, what we really have so far is:

	A	X	X	Transition		A
	I	III		(I)	V	I
m.	17	62	89	114	122	123

What, then, should we expect of the passage to come now? From the point of view of the pattern just outlined, it might well be a coda. From the point of view of the original, though by now somewhat discredited, sonata form, it should represent the second theme. In fact, it serves both functions:

140–53   Harmonically, an extended I–V–I cadence, repeated and then extended. Thus it would seem to be coda material. But the rhythmic element of the dotted motif is a clear reference to the second theme.

154–59   Interruption by the famous alternation of the chords of D♭ major and G minor, which continue the characteristic dotted rhythm. Here Berlioz is telescoping the relationship previously set up. He then reduces the opposition of the two poles by his typical device of progressive reinterpretation: the D♭ (C♯) is retained in the flutes while the harmonies containing it constantly change. (Compare the treatment of the A♭ in the bass at I, mm. 49–59). At its last appearance, the C♯ is a member of the augmented sixth leading back to V.[2]

160–64   Continuation of the interrupted cadence, which, by its contour, suggests the cadence at the end of the exposition.

164–68   A sudden turn to the dominant, and the beginning of the *idée fixe* in the clarinet.

169   The clarinet suggested G major, but it is interrupted by a peremptory G minor.

170–78   But now G major returns for the concluding chords.

Can we find any relationship between the March and the preceding movements? If we can, we have disposed of the chief argument of those who claim that the symphony was not a unitary conception but a concatenation of previously composed pieces. We cannot call on the presence of the *idée fixe* to help us, since the manuscript suggests that this, like so

2. For another interpretation of this passage, see Heinrich Schenker, *Harmonie-lehre*, Stuttgart and Berlin, 1906, pp. 147–48. Schenker neither admires the passage nor approves of Schumann's remarks about it.

Ex. 12.

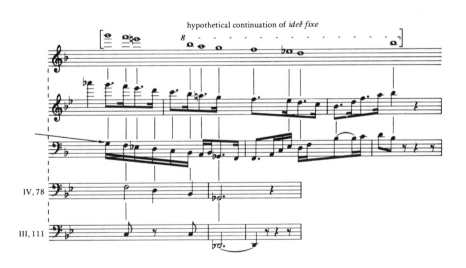

hypothetical continuation of *ideé fixe*

many other ideas in the symphony, was an afterthought. But the passage
we have dubbed X offers a clue. It is in B♭, a key that has been exploited
only once before, in the central section of the third movement. Once we
start looking for correspondences between these two passages, they seem
too numerous to be coincidental: the resemblance of Theme B of the
present movement to the bass recitative and to the beginning of the *idée
fixe*; the climax in each case on a high A♭; the striking descent to a low
G♭—a G♭ which, in the March, is reached through the descending major
seventh already familiar. Example 12 outlines these connections. They
suggest that, even though the March was originally designed for *Les
Francs-juges*, during the composition of the opera the symphony was
already taking subconscious shape in the composer's musical imagination.
By placing the March in the symphony, Berlioz acknowledged an underlying and pervasive relationship. (See also Example 13, which suggests
further elements common to the *idée fixe*, the March, and the Finale.)

FIFTH MOVEMENT: *Songe d'une nuit du sabbat*

The finale naturally returns to the C major-minor of the first movement, and like that movement it has an elaborate introduction. Although
different in materials and mood, the present introduction is clearly
related to the first one. The following analysis indicates certain obvious
parallels:

Finale		*First Movement*	
1–20	An upbeat *section* prepares for the entrance of the tonic at m. 19. Two phrases, in free sequence, mm. 1–11 and mm. 12–20.	1–2	An upbeat *measure* prepares for the tonic at m. 2.
21–28	Theme in I (major), moving to V, interrupted by an outburst on III. The theme is, of course, a final transformation of the *idée fixe*, parodied by the clarinet.	3–17	Theme in I (minor), moving to V and then to III. The theme dissolves into a transition (VI–V) to the next section.
29–39	Interlude moving III–VII (V of III).	18–27	Interlude moving I (major-minor) to VII (V of III).
40–64	Repetition of theme in III, now complete, in clarinet and piccolo, leading to:	29–35	Variation of theme, beginning in III, moving through V to:

| 65–69 | I–VI. |
| 70–101 | Elaboration of VI–V–I (minor). At mm. 76–78 and mm. 84–85, the first hints of what is to become the fugue subject. |

| 36–48 | I–VI. |
| 49–72 | Elaboration of VI–V–I (major). |

If the above correspondence is significant, then what follows in the finale—viz., the *Dies irae*—should be in some way analogous to the first theme of a sonata allegro. Now, in one sense the *Dies irae* is still part of the introduction: it is still in C minor; although notated in the tempo and meter of the main movement (Allegro, $\frac{6}{8}$), it has not achieved the eighth-note motion that will be typical; and it ends with a more complete build-up of the dominant than any that precedes it. But from another point of view, the *Dies irae* must be considered as an integral part of the formal scheme—a kind of "first theme"—since the recapitulatory section of the movement to come will include it in contrapuntal combination with the other main idea. So, as in the March, there is an ambiguity of form at work. It may therefore be no accident that the *Dies irae* is accompanied by an ostinato (in the bells) based on the same C-G fourth that underlay so much of the *idée fixe* when it was exposed as a "first theme." This fourth, together with another hint of the fugato to come, is used to form a little introduction within this section:

102–26	Introduction to *Dies irae*.
127–47	First phrase, melody in bassoons and ophicleides in dotted halves.
147–57	Same phrase in horns and trombones, in dotted quarters.
157–62	Same phrase in woodwinds, in quarters and eighths.
163–86	Second phrase, undergoing the same successive treatment.
187–221	Third phrase, undergoing the same successive treatment.
222–40	Preparation for the sabbath round, with crescendo to V.

The fact that the sabbath round now enters with a thoroughgoing fugal exposition is one more reason why everything that precedes it sounds introductory. If we have now, at last, entered upon the movement proper, its broad outlines may be indicated thus:

241–69	Exposition: I, V, and I.
269–88	Episode: I moving to III♭, then VI♭ to V of V.
289–305	Partial counterexposition: V and I.
305–406	Development, to which *Dies irae* is added. III♭ moving eventually to V.
407–35	Joint recapitulation of fugue subject and *Dies irae:* I, V, I to VI.

435–47 Transition: VI to V of VI.
448–60 Augmentation of fugue subject: VI to II.
480–524 New version of fugue subject, interrupted by the *Dies irae*; and
final cadence: I, IV (minor), V–I.

The fugal theme is a twofold presentation of the chain of descending thirds familiar from the first movement. (Is it related to the *idée fixe* as well? Perhaps, but it also shows similarities to other themes. See examples 11 and 13.) Two motifs are to be singled out later for special treatment. The first (X) is an ascending upbeat figure that, as Example 13 shows, already undergoes development during the course of the theme itself. The other (Y) is a syncopated motif that marks the end of the subject.

Ex. 13.

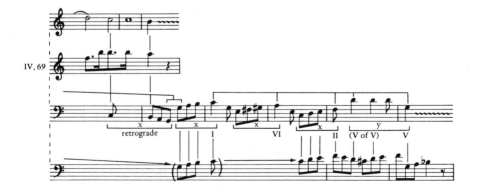

The first statement is already accompanied by two countersubjects; but since these overlap by only one eighth, they can best be considered as one continuous idea. (See Schumann's Ex. 10, p. 241. The countersubject is given as a single line in the right hand, mm. 3–6.) In the following sketch of the exposition, S=Subject, A=Answer, CS=Countersubject. Although many of the parts are doubled by the winds, only strings are indicated. An interesting symmetry results:

Violins I		CS	S	CS
Violins II	CS		CS	
Violas	CS	A	CS	A
Cellos, Basses	S	CS		CS
m.	241	248	255	262
	I	V	I	V

The episode that follows is in two phases:

269–78 A sequence based on X and Y against descending scales, moving I–V, VII–IV.

279–88 A descending half-step motif is developed both in detail and in the motion from one measure to the next. The motif is then inverted, yielding a chromatic rise which ends as III♭–VI♭, leading to V of V.

A partial counterexposition, reversing subject and answer, now occurs. It is introduced by an abortive stretto:

Winds	Incomplete Theme	CS	CS
Violins			S
Cellos, Basses		A	
m.	289	291	298
	V minor	V major	I

A long development is now introduced by a turn toward III♭ in m. 305. It is almost as if everything since m. 286 (also III♭) were parenthetical.

305–09   The impression that this section is a continuation of the first episode after an interruption is supported by the similarity of musical material. Brass chords are answered by reiterations of the descending half step (woodwinds) against a truncated form of X (strings) ; III♭.

310–14   A sequence of the same, V minor.

315–19   A varied sequence, VI♭.

320–27   The suggestion of another sequence (on N?) turns instead into a 6-measure extension, on the descending half-step motif, of VII♭ minor. The seventh measure uses the same motif for a sudden and crucial change of direction: VII♭ minor to VI major. At this point we realize that this movement, too, exploits the contrast of the major and minor sixth degree that we have found so characteristic of the symphony.

327–62   The first two measures, moving to G minor, show the goal of this passage: the dominant. Especially to be noted here is the use of the rhythm and contour of the fugue subject, first in arpeggios (mm. 331 ff., in the lower strings imitated by the bassoons), and then in chromatic scales (mm. 355 ff., violas). Again we hear the alternation of the two forms of mm. 338–40 (A♭), and m. 341 (A♮ again). When the *Dies irae* returns in m. 348, it, too, shows an indecision between the two notes!

363–406   The *Dies irae* breaks off as the bass drum enters. The next note of the theme would have been G, and that is the way we interpret the drum roll. (And that is the way Liszt transcribed it, misleading Schumann.) The long dominant build-up exploits the form of the subject heard in mm. 355–58 leading to a climax that extends Y through 8 measures. Now follow four attempts to get the recapitulation under way; only the last succeeds.

If my suggestion as to the parenthetical nature of the counterexposition is right—and the similar situation of the recapitulated second theme at I, mm. 193–200, supports this view—then the tonic return of the fugue subject rounds off a huge I–III♭–V–I cycle. The texture here is homophonic; nay, almost monophonic. The dominant answer (m. 414) shows why: Berlioz does not wish to distract us from his tour de force—the combination of the fugue subject with the *Dies irae*. As Schumann points out, the former soon gives out and resorts to swirling scales. In order to make the combination work, Berlioz chose a transposition of the plainchant beginning on C; its second phrase accordingly moves from I to VI for a cadence in A minor.

This key, after a short transition (I–V in A minor), sustains an almost complete augmentation of the fugue subject (mm. 448–60) in violas and woodwinds. The following passage (mm. 460–79) elaborates the progression II–V, revealing the entire recapitulation from m. 407 on as a huge I–V–I–VI–II–V. This is precisely the harmonic progression outlined by the fugue subject itself! (See the chords suggested in Ex. 13.)

The final expansion of the tonic once more brings together the two chief ideas of the movement:

480–84   A passage obviously representing the fugue subject; its derivation is shown in Example 13. It is accompanied by X on every eighth-note beat. Harmonically, it moves from I through a diminished seventh toward IV.

485–95   An expansion of IV–V, presenting the beginning of the *Dies irae* in the successive diminutions of the introduction. IV is minor here, and it is through a bass progression of A♭–G that we move to V.

496–524 The ending is firmly and unmistakably in major, but even here the III♭ obtrudes itself into the cadence (mm. 508–09). Even more remarkable is the way that the alternation of A♭ and A♮ is carried through almost to the end. Indeed, are not mm. 504–06 a direct reference to the *idée fixe*? (See Ex. 14.)

Ex. 14.

In the foregoing discussion I have tried to emphasize the connections among the various movements in the hope of establishing the *Fantastic Symphony* as a unified whole. Such a conception of the work must depend less on the exact quotations of the *idée fixe*, which could after all be worked more or less mechanically into almost any context, than on harmonic and tonal relationships, motivic reminiscences, and pervading melodic patterns. I fully realize that apparent evidence of this kind often conceals pitfalls for the unwary. It is true, for example, that the contrast between the major and minor sixths is a constant feature of this symphony. But it is equally true, as a glance at other works by Berlioz will show, that this motif is a hallmark of his melodic style. Examples 15a, b, and c, are drawn respectively from the *Requiem, Romeo and Juliet,* and

Ex. 15.

The Damnation of Faust. Each one exhibits, in transposition, the A♭–G, A♮–G of the *Fantastic.* So perhaps all that this bit of tune detecting has revealed is that the symphony is really by Berlioz. Yet the multiplicity of these details and similar ones (which I have by no means exhausted), supported as they are by pervasive harmonic and tonal patterns, is impressive. There is of course only one way to decide whether the symphony makes sense as a whole. As Schumann succinctly put it, "Enough of this—one must now hear the work."

VIEWS AND COMMENTS
BY COMPOSERS

Unless specified otherwise, all numbered footnotes in the following essays are those of the authors.

FELIX MENDELSSOHN

~~~

[*A Letter from Rome*] †

During the years 1830–32 Felix Mendelssohn (1809–37) traveled extensively; his letters to his family offer us first-hand knowledge both of his
personality and of the musical life of the day. In Italy he met Berlioz,
who had recently arrived there as a result of winning the Prix de Rome.
The following extract is from a letter to his mother dated March 15,
1831. (For Berlioz's account of their meeting, see *Memoirs,* pp. 290–95.)

* * *

But now you shall hear about Berlioz and his music. He makes me sad,
because he is really a cultured, agreeable man and yet composes so very
badly.

The day after tomorrow he is going back to Paris. He seems terribly
in love, and this has been the inspiration for a symphony which he calls
Épisode de la vie d'un artiste. When it was performed, 2000 copies of
explanatory notes were distributed. In them he says that the composer
has imagined the theme of the first movement as depicting a charming
young lady who has fascinated the artist, and that his rage, jealousy, tenderness and tears are pictured in it. The second movement describes a
ball where everything seems empty to him because she is missing. The
third is called *scène aux champs;* the cowherds play a *ranz des vaches,* the
instruments imitating the rustle of the leaves (all this in the printed program). Fear and hope are mixed in the artist's soul. Before the fourth
movement (so continues the program), the artist, having poisoned himself with opium but misjudged the quantity, instead of dying has the
most horrible visions. The fourth movement is just such a vision where
he is present at his own execution; it is called *marche au supplice.* The
fifth and last is called *songe d'une nuit du sabbat,* in which he sees the

witches dancing on the Blocksberg, his beloved among them. At the same time he hears the distorted *cantus firmus* of the "Dies Irae," to which the witches are dancing.

How utterly loathsome all this is to me, I don't have to tell you. To see one's most cherished ideas debased and expressed in perverted caricatures would enrage anyone. And yet this is only the program. The execution is still more miserable: nowhere a spark, no warmth, utter foolishness, contrived passion represented through every possible exaggerated orchestral means: four timpani, two pianos for four hands, which are supposed to imitate bells, two harps, many big drums, violins divided into eight parts, two parts for the double basses which play solo passages, and all these means (to which I would not object if they were properly employed) used to express nothing but indifferent drivel, mere grunting, shouting, screaming back and forth. And when you see the composer himself, that friendly, quiet, meditative person, calmly and assuredly going his way, never for a moment in doubt of his vocation, unable to listen to any outside voice, since he wishes to follow only his inner inspiration, when you see how keenly and correctly he evaluates and recognizes everything, yet is in complete darkness about himself—it is unspeakably dreadful, and I cannot express how deeply the sight of him depresses me. I have not been able to work for two days.

* * *

FRANZ LISZT

A Berlioz Concert †

Franz Liszt (1811–86) attended the première of the *Fantastic Symphony* and forthwith became Berlioz's friend and champion. The following is an example of his support.

True, most of Liszt's literary output must be viewed with suspicion. It is well known, for example, that Princess Sayn-Wittgenstein, with whom he lived for many years, played much more than the part of a mere stenographer in the preparation of his *Life of Chopin* and other writings. It should therefore come as no surprise that an article in *Le Monde*, December 11, 1836, although signed by Liszt, was probably composed

† *Le Monde*, December 11, 1836. Translation by the editor.

—in whole or in part—by the Countess d'Agoult ("Daniel Stern"), the authoress who was to become the mother of Liszt's children. Such, at any rate, is the implication of a letter he wrote to her shortly thereafter.[1] Nevertheless, we may assume that the essay, a review of a concert at the Conservatory that included both the *Fantastic Symphony* and *Harold in Italy*, expounded Liszt's views to his satisfaction.

* * * Here, indeed, is a spectacle worthy of attention and one well calculated to restore the flagging spirits and the yielding will power of the composer whose first hearing fails to arouse the plaudits of the crowd: the sight of Berlioz spending his entire early youth in bodily combat, so to speak, with an uncomprehending public; responding with undaunted perseverance to coarse sarcasm, unintelligent prejudice, and peremptory condemnation; walking on like the philosopher who thus answered those who denied the possibility of motion[2]; and offering as his sole argument the performance of his works, by an orchestra increasingly well rehearsed—works that the flood of critical grumbling lifted ever higher, like a noble three-master riding out a storm.

The public complained that its patience was giving out; nevertheless, attracted as if in its own despite by the power of genius, the public kept coming back. Then, little by little, from the midst of the crowd that had almost universally condemned, there arose here and there a few individual opinions, a few voices isolated at first, but soon surrounded by partisans of the more timid sort, who are always seeking support. Thus arose a second public, as eager to defend Berlioz as the first had been to attack him. Today sarcasm and mockery are out; even the terms of the argument are different: now the question is whether the composer of the *Fantastic Symphony* is merely a talented composer or a real genius.

For us there can be no doubt. "Genius," said Buffon,[3] "is patience." Under this rubric, who could refuse the title to Berlioz? But, leaving aside this definition as more academic than accurate, we say the following: genius is greatness in novelty; genius is thought creating its own form; it is the sense of the infinite revealed in the finite. Now, what musical works manifest boldness of innovation, profundity of thought, and wealth of forms to a higher degree than *Harold* and *Épisode de la vie d'un artiste*? How can one deny abundance and diversity of ideas to the composer who, in a single work, could depict equally well the *vague des*

1. See *La Correspondance de Liszt et de Madame d'Agoult*, ed. by Daniel Olliver, Paris, 1933, p. 193.

2. This practical refutation of the Eleatic theory that all motion is impossible is attributed to Diogenes the Cynic. (See Simplicius's *Commentary on Aristotle's Physics*. I am indebted to Prof. Gregory Vlastos for this reference.) [*Editor*]

3. Georges Louis Leclerc, Comte de Buffon (1707–88), French naturalist. [*Editor*]

passions, the intoxication of a ball, the mysterious harmonies of nature, the terrors of an execution, and could then transport us into the midst of a sabbath, where we find the dismal fantasy of Macbeth's witches conjoined with the satanic orgies of the Brocken?[4]

To these eminent gifts as painter and poet let us now add an undeniable knowledge of instrumentation—a knowledge Berlioz gained with difficulty, by the sweat of his brow, at a time when his musical vocation, opposed by his family, had reduced him to a state of proud poverty, when he would sit unobserved in the dark recesses of a theater orchestra. If we carefully examine these new combinations, these striking effects, whose secret seemed known only to Meyerbeer,—then it appears to us impossible not to accord Berlioz a pre-eminent position. There are those who point in objection to the small number of his compositions; we ask them whether Beethoven would have been considered only an ordinary musician if he had died immediately after writing his Fifth Symphony. Notwithstanding, we shall pray no less heartily for Berlioz's early appearance on the operatic stage, for only there can he display his great abilities freely and without shackles; only there will success bestow on his works a splendor that nonoperatic compositions can never achieve.[5] * * *

RICHARD WAGNER

[*On Berlioz and the Fantastic Symphony*] †

During the year 1841, while Richard Wagner (1813–83) was residing in Paris, he wrote periodical reports of the musical life there for the *Dresdener Abendzeitung*. An expression of Wagner's later opinion of Berlioz can be found in his *Oper und Drama* (1851).

It is becoming clear to me that I shall finally have to seize an occasion to speak of Berlioz, since I realize that the opportunity will not present

4. A mountain in Saxony, long a site of pagan worship, and hence the legendary scene of the revelries of Walpurgis Night. The reference here is probably to the famous Brocken episode in Goethe's *Faust*. [*Editor*]

5. Berlioz had already begun work on his first completed opera, *Benvenuto Cellini*, which was finished and performed in 1838. [*Editor*]

† *Dresdener Abendzeitung*, May 5, 1841. Translation by the editor.

itself in due course. The fact that, in reviewing the daily events of the Parisian world of entertainment (or, if you prefer, of art), no chance has arisen for me to discuss this musician of genius—this very fact seems to me symptomatic and offers me a good way to introduce my opinions on Berlioz, who in any case has the right to demand that I devote to him a page of special importance in my reports from Paris.

Berlioz is not the kind of composer who just happens in due course, and so I cannot just happen on an opportunity of discussing him. He is not connected with those ostentatious, snobbish institutions of the Parisian art world and has nothing to do with them; both Opera and Conservatory shut their doors against him with astonishing speed after his first appearance. Berlioz has been forced to become and to remain a resolute exception to long-standing rule, and this he has indeed become and remains through and through. Whoever wishes to hear his music must go for this purpose to Berlioz himself, for nowhere else will he find any of it, not even where one can encounter Mozart next to Musard.[1] One hears Berlioz's compositions only at those concerts that he gives once or twice a year. These remain his exclusive domain; here he has his works played by an orchestra that he himself has specially trained, before a public that he has conquered in a ten-year campaign. Nowhere else can one hear anything by Berlioz, save at those politico-musical state ceremonies, in street or church, to which he is occasionally summoned.[2]

This lonely isolation of Berlioz's, however, not only envelops his position in the outer world, but also permeates his inner life and underlies its evolution. No matter how French he is, no matter how much his nature and his aims sympathize with those of his countrymen—he nevertheless stands alone. He sees no one before him on whom he can count for support, no one near him on whom he can lean. From our Germany the spirit of Beethoven has wafted over to him, and there must have been times when Berlioz wished he were German; it was at such times that his genius urged him to write as the great master wrote, to express what he felt Beethoven's works expressed. But whenever he picked up his pen, his French blood naturally welled up again, the same blood that bubbled in Auber's veins when he wrote the volcanic last act of his *Muette*[3]—happy

1. Philippe Musard (1793–1859), French composer of dance music, known as *le roi des quadrilles.* Berlioz called him *"le Mozart de la contredanse."* [*Editor*]

2. E.g. the performance of the Requiem in the Invalides (Dec. 5, 1837), and that of the *Funeral and Triumphal Symphony* at an open-air procession and service (July 28, 1840). Both occasions commemorated the Revolution of 1830. [*Editor*]

3. *La Muette de Portici* (or *Masaniello*), celebrated opera by Daniel-François-Esprit Auber (1782–1871). The huge success of its production in Paris in 1828 paved the way for the vogue of grand opera. [*Editor*]

Auber, who did not know Beethoven's symphonies! But Berlioz knew them, nay, he understood them; they had inspired him, they had intoxicated his spirit—and yet he could not forget that French blood flowed in his veins. Then he felt that he could not become another Beethoven, but he also realized that he could not write like Auber. He became Berlioz and wrote his *Fantastic Symphony*, a work that would have made Beethoven smile, just as Auber smiles at it, but one that could send Paganini into a feverish ecstasy of excitement and could win for its creator a party of supporters who will listen to no music in the world but the *Fantastic Symphony* of Berlioz.

No one who hears this symphony here in Paris, played by Berlioz's orchestra, can help believing that he is hearing a marvel without precedent. From the vast inner realm of a heroically strong imagination erupts a shower of passions as if from a volcano; what we see are gigantic clouds of smoke, separated and modeled into fleeting shapes only by lightning and streaks of flame. Everything is monstrous, bold, but endlessly painful. Nowhere is beauty of form to be encountered, nowhere that majestic stream to whose calm, assured flow we would entrust ourselves in confident expectation. The first movement of Beethoven's Fifth Symphony would seem an act of pure kindness to me after the *Fantastic Symphony*.

I said that the French tendency prevails even in Berlioz; in fact, were this not the case, and were it possible for him to depart from it, then we might gain in him what we Germans would consider a worthy follower of Beethoven. But that tendency bars him from a direct approach to Beethoven's genius. It is the tendency to look abroad, to try to find sympathetic resonances in extreme situations. At those times when the German prefers to withdraw from social life in order to explore the sources of his creative energy in his own inner being, we see the Frenchman, on the contrary, searching for those sources by climbing the most distant peaks of society. The Frenchman, whose first purpose is to entertain, seeks the perfection of his art in ennobling, in spiritualizing this entertainment; but he always keeps before his eyes its immediate goal, i.e. to please, and to capture as many listeners as possible. Thus the "effect," the momentary impression, is the chief thing for him, and remains such. If he completely lacks the power of inner vision, the attainment of this goal is enough to satisfy him; but if he is gifted with real creative force, he makes use of this "effect," to be sure, but only as the first and most important means of expressing his inner vision.

What a schism must now occur in the soul of an artist like Berlioz!

On the one hand a vital power of inner vision impels him to tap the deepest, most mysterious springs of thought as sources of his art; while on the other hand both the characteristic demands of his countrymen, among whom he belongs and whose sympathies he shares, and his own artistic inclinations to boot urge him to give primary expression only to his most superficial creative impulses. He feels that he has something extraordinary, something lasting to say, for which Auber's language is much too restricted, but that his own language must sound something like it in order to win from the outset an immediate public. And thus he falls into that devilishly confused musical idiom, striking in its novelty, with which he stuns and wins over the gaping mob, while he scares off those who could have understood his meaning from within, but who scorn to take the trouble of feeling their way in from without.

It is also unfortunate that Berlioz seems to enjoy his isolation and stubbornly tries to maintain it. He has no friend whom he considers worthy of asking for advice, or whom he would allow to point out this or that defect in his works.

* * * Therefore Berlioz will remain forever incomplete and perhaps really shine only as a transient, marvelous exception.

And that is too bad! If Berlioz could appropriate the many excellent qualities that characterize the latest brilliant period of modern French music, if he could give up his so arrogantly maintained isolation and avail himself of any valid musical style, present or past, as a foundation for building his own, then he would surely acquire such powerful influence over France's musical future that his memory would last forever.* * *

CHARLES GOUNOD

[Berlioz] †

Charles François Gounod (1818–93) knew Berlioz personally and admired his music. The essay from which this extract has been taken first appeared

† From *Composers on Music,* ed. by Sam Morgenstern. Copyright 1956 by Pantheon Books, Inc. Reprinted by permission of Pantheon Books, a division of Random House, Inc., and Faber and Faber Ltd. Translation by Mr. Morgenstern.

as an introduction to Berlioz's *Lettres intimes* (Paris, 1882) . It was later re-printed in Gounod's *Mémoires d'un artiste* (Paris, 1896) .

* * * Berlioz was a man all of a piece, a whole man who admitted nei-ther to concessions nor transactions. He belonged to the race of Alceste; hence, the race of Oronte[1] was naturally against him, and of Orontes there are, God knows, quite a few! People found him ill-tempered, sullen, biting, and what not! But along with his sensitivity, heightened to the point of irascibility, we must consider all the irritating, embittering experiences, all the personal misfortunes and the thousand and one set-backs and rejections endured by this proud spirit, incapable of any base desire to please or of cowardly, low fawning.

If his criticisms seemed all too severe to those whom they touched, at least it could never be said that his motive was jealousy, so incompatible with his noble, generous and loyal nature.

The trials Berlioz had to undergo as a contestant for the *grand prix de Rome* were the prophetic prelude to those he had to meet throughout the rest of his career. He competed four times and obtained the prize only at the age of twenty-seven, in 1830, by dint of perseverance and in spite of all sorts of obstacles which he had to surmount. In the very same year that he carried off the prize with his cantata, *Sardanapale,* he had a work performed which showed how far his artistry had developed from the standpoint of conception, color and technical mastery. His *Symphonie fantastique (An Episode in the Life of an Artist)* was a veritable musical event, the importance of which may be gauged by the fanatic adherence of some and the violent opposition of others. However, no matter how much one might argue about such a composition, it reveals, in the young man who produced it, the very highest faculties of inven-tion and a powerful poetic feeling which one rediscovers in all his works. Berlioz hurled into musical circulation a multitude of effects and orches-tral combinations unknown before him and which even the most illus-trious musicians have not hesitated to make their own. He revolutionized the domain of instrumentation, and in this respect at least, he can be said to have created a "school." And yet, despite the brilliant triumphs, in France as well as abroad, Berlioz was under attack all his life. Although his personal direction as an eminent orchestral conductor and his indefatigable energy added so many elements of clarity and chances for success to performances, he never had more than a limited and re-strained public. He lacked the "public," that "everybody" which makes

1. Two characters in Molière's *Le Misanthrope.* Alceste, the hero, is a man of ruthless sincerity and utter integrity. Oronte is a conceited man of the world. [*Editor*]

success *popular*. His *Les Troyens*, which he had foreseen as being the source of all his sorrows, truly finished him. It can be said of him, as of his heroic namesake, Hector, that he perished under the walls of Troy.

With Berlioz all impressions, all sensations—whether joyful or sad—are expressed in extremes, at the point of delirium. As he himself says, he is a "volcano." Our sensitivity carries us equally far in sorrow and joy: Tabor and Golgotha are related. Happiness does not consist of the absence of suffering, anymore than genius consists of the absence of faults.

The great geniuses suffer and must suffer, but they need not complain; they have known intoxication unknown to the rest of men and, if they have wept tears of sadness, they have poured tears of ineffable joy. That in itself is a heaven for which one never pays what it is worth. * * *

HUGO WOLF

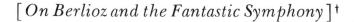

[*On Berlioz and the Fantastic Symphony*]†

Hugo Wolf (1860–1903) reviewed concerts for the weekly *Wiener Salon-blatt* from 1884 to 1887. A performance of the *Fantastic Symphony* by the Vienna Philharmonic Orchestra gave him a chance to advance the cause of Berlioz, to praise Schumann as a critic, and to excoriate the Viennese public—especially the last.

Whatever may have moved the Philharmonic to take an exception and abstain for once from its tried and true tactics against Berlioz's music, we will not inquire further into the mysterious motivations that accomplished this miracle. Enough that for this once the orchestra did not just stop at the announcement but actually came up with a performance of the *Symphonie fantastique*. I can dispense with an analysis of this work, no less gigantic in execution than in design, all the more readily since on the one hand it can be assumed that Schumann's well-known critique is familiar to every music lover, and since on the other hand the meager

† *Wiener Salonblatt*, April 5, 1885. Translation by the editor.

success the work enjoyed at the recent concert requires a deeper examination of the attitude of our concert-goers, both in general and in particular. Before I take up the attack on this subject (and an attack it shall be, depend on that!), let me refer once more to Robert Schumann's splendid essay.

Schumann's unprejudiced point of view toward Berlioz's work, his intimate understanding of its poetic content, his acute analysis of both its formal and its musical aspects (which has furnished a model of what musical criticism should be), and lastly the ungrudging appreciation that enabled him to recognize in Berlioz's procedures, arisen from innermost necessity, a decisive step forward for instrumental music—all this does credit to Schumann the critic no less than to Schumann the composer. One should bear in mind still further that when Schumann wrote this critique, as fair as it is witty and lucid, he was unable to turn even once to the score for support, but had to base his opinions on a piano transcription—albeit one by Liszt. To be sure, this would have been of little significance in the case of other composers, but it is of the highest importance for a musician like Berlioz; for whereas in a transcription the notes of his music resemble dried-up mummies, the scores of this master remind one of Prosper Alpanus's books of magic in *Klein Zaches*,[1] for in them note heads and stems, dots and rests, clefs and bar lines lead a ghostly life of their own. Nevertheless Schumann recognized at first sight the beauties, the colossal dimensions, the bold strokes, the brilliant developments, the depths of feeling, the power of thought, the pregnancy of expression, the mastery of form, the constructive logic of this spiky problem child of Berlioz's muse. But when he encountered passages where all this was perforce concealed from him, he did not thereupon cry murder, nor did he wrap his perplexity in the cloak of critical authority (that tattered cloak, through whose holes the vanity and ignorance of our ephemerally powerful critics grin repulsively at the world); rather, having arrived at the end of his investigation, he openly admitted that, *without a score*, the last pages of the symphony must be considered poor. Indeed, one could hardly find any admirer of Berlioz's compositions to whom the fifth movement of the *Fantastic Symphony* would appeal *as a piano transcription*. The orchestral effect of this movement, with the *Dies irae* cantus firmus in the trombones and the witches' sabbath circling above it, is of course overwhelming, shattering, annihilating; but the original bears the same relation to the transcription as a real hurricane to one

---

1. A fantastic tale (1819) by E. T. A. Hoffmann (1776-1822). Prosper Alpanus is a benevolent magician who figures prominently in the story. [*Editor*]

badly painted or described, as you will.

One can deduce how seriously Schumann took his critical mission from his own words, for example these: "In the firm conviction that certain academic theorists" (doesn't one think immediately of the bullfighters of our contemporary criticism?) "have done much more harm than our heaven-storming practical musicians, and the protection of wretched mediocrity" (doesn't one here think involuntarily of our well-known but unfortunately old-fashioned symphonists of today?) "has caused more mischief than any commendation awarded to poetical extravagance, we call once and for all on posterity to be our witness: in the case of Berlioz's compositions we have not postponed our critical wisdom for ten years, as is usual, but have stated, in anticipation, that *genius* burns in this Frenchman."[2] Oh, how much do I honour, how much do I revere Schumann, even were it only for the sake of this one critique!

Now to the attack! I mentioned at the beginning of this essay that the majority of the public turned a deaf ear to the Berlioz symphony. I now ask: Does our concert public deserve to hear anything besides Diabelli's children's pieces or Brahms's symphonies and concertos?[3] Don't these two masters completely suffice to satisfy the musical needs of our concert public? If one wants to arouse in the public gentle emotions, quiet joy, tender longing—one plays Diabelli. If the public wants to suffer attacks of asceticism, to be put into a melancholy mood, to be able to indulge in despair—one plays Brahms. If, against all expectation, the compositions of these two famous followers of Beethoven should excite the reverse emotions in the public—that's fine too. Suppose that Master Brahms should flatter the cheerfully disposed heart, or Master Diabelli should upset one's stomach—what difference would that make? But Hector Berlioz (notice that I dare not apply the euphemism "Master" to this composer, however much it might advance him in the public eye) —what can the oversensitive, distingué Viennese concert public make of this prickly hedgehog? Has he normal human feelings? Is his art pure? Does he recognize law and order? Are his means of expression comprehensible? Isn't his world the tomb of all reason, of all sound human intelligence? Oh, yes! Yes, indeed!

And now for the rejoinder. "Has Berlioz normal feelings?" What folly! Do you believe that the eternally dancing circle of those

2. From Schumann's article on the Overture to *Les Francs-juges*, 1836. [Editor]
3. Anton Diabelli (1781–1858), Austrian composer and music publisher, is known to us today primarily as the composer of the theme of a famous set of variations. It may seem surprising to find his name linked with that of Brahms, but Wolf had a notorious deaf spot where the latter was concerned. [*Editor*]

holy spirits who, speaking in voices of thunder from the shining aureole
of divinity, reveal to the inspired artist's clairvoyant, miracle-craving eye
things never before heard, never seen, never dreamt, never imagined—do
you believe that they must wear your misshapen forms, proclaim in your
squeaky voices, carry your minuscule clockwork ticking in their breasts?
Who are you, that you presume to dispute with the divine? If your eyes
are weak, your minds bemused, and your heads twisted, must the artist's
(to be sure, not the "Master's") therefore be the same? Do you believe
that *your* Beethoven wrote his melodies straight from *your* hearts? That
would indeed be jolly. You, the Philharmonic concert public, have *never*
grasped him, *never* felt him, *never* understood him. You have chewed
him like cud, then spit him up and chewed him again, so long as you
have imagined that he tastes good. But he *doesn't* taste good to you, and if
Vienna's glorious critics should lead you astray (and why shouldn't
they?), saying that Beethoven is actually a wretched composer, that he
offers most unwholesome spiritual food, you would give the matter no
thought (or else I'm a Chinaman), but would straightway vomit and
refuse to hear any more Beethoven.

"Is Berlioz's art pure?"

Isn't the concept of purity one that has long since escaped you? You
whose views and tastes have been formed by the shower of frivolous
French novels, of shallow French conversation pieces, you who are so
pure that you wish to drape the Venus of Medici or of Milo, but only
because naked beauty leaves you untouched, because your blunted senses
are no longer capable of natural reactions, because only vulgarity titil-
lates you, because you are, in a word, impure—how can you venture to
raise such a question at all?

"Does Berlioz observe law and order?"

Now, how do such highly ingenious objections occur to you clever
ones? Aren't you beasts of burden, doing your job from one day to the
next in a dull stupor, either pampered and supported, or downtrodden,
pushed about, and enslaved, by the good or ill will of circumstance? And
have you ever taken the trouble to give really serious consideration to
law and order? Do you know any other order than police order, or any
other law than the fear of fine or imprisonment? But the comet of genius
won't confine its course to customary paths. It creates order and promotes
its own will into law. And Berlioz is a genius. Bow before him, you wise
ladies and gentlemen and you critics; be henceforth modest and don't
imagine that, because the eagle in the highest heavens is aware of you,
you must by the same token see him.

"Are Berlioz's means of expression comprehensible?"

Certainly not to fools.

"Isn't his artistic world the tomb of all sound reason and intelligence?"

Ah! If only all Berlioz's opponents could be buried in this tomb, if only they might completely lose their damned reason and their accursed intelligence! For the mischief that clever men contrive, especially when they take up aesthetics on the side and also, alas, act as critics, would try the patience of a Job.

The Philharmonic has finally pulled itself together to do something; unfortunately, because of its conservative position, it must bear the blame for a large share in the miseducation of our concert public. We hope that it will not disdain the applause of the young people who, from standing room and gallery, gleefully responded to the splendid performance no less than to the magnificent composition. In really important matters, the young have always been in the forefront. Let us not allow the dribble and the downright dishonesty of our critical opponents to lead us astray. We bear the shield of truth to protect ourselves, we wield the sword of enthusiasm to wound our opponents; and henceforth may our watchword be: *War on the Philistines, War on the Critics!*

CAMILLE SAINT-SAËNS

[*The Fantastic Symphony*] †

During his long life Camille Saint-Saëns (1835–1921) had many occasions to pay tribute to Berlioz, whom he considered one of the great geniuses of French music. This extract is from an essay written shortly before Saint-Saëns's death, at the age of eighty-six, in 1921.

* * * Let us speak first of the *Symphonie fantastique*. It has remained in the concert repertory; but, to judge its value, one must consider the time

† From *Le Ménestrel*, Vol. 83, No. 42 (October 21, 1921), Heugel & Co., publishers. Translated by the editor and reprinted by permission of the publishers.

when it was written, one must understand just how it differed, by its nature, by its very dimensions, from all previous symphonies, and realize what a prodigious flight of inspiration, what intrepid audacity it presupposed!

Beethoven alone had previously given a program to a symphony: the *Pastoral*.[1] But in the present example, it is not merely a case of painting a natural landscape with peasants: the composer places himself on stage.

He depicts his passion for an ideal woman, a ball where he meets her, a rural scene in which, to the murmur of distant thunder, the image of the dear one appears to him. Then, without our knowing why, he kills the well-beloved and is condemned to death. Finally we see him in Hell, where the adored woman is met again, dishonored and ludicrous, in the midst of a sabbath.

And from all this arises an admirable work, completely original in style, in sonority, in every constituent factor, and utterly different from anything that had been previously conceived and executed.

If the program, with its exaggerated romanticism, has passed out of fashion, the musical work has held up; it is still as young, as astounding, as on its first day. * * *

VIRGIL THOMSON

~~~

The Berlioz Case †

Virgil Thomson (1896–) was chief music critic of the New York *Herald Tribune* from 1940 to 1954. The article from which this excerpt was taken appeared on October 11, 1942, in anticipation of a performance of *The Damnation of Faust.*

* * *

The undisputed facts about Berlioz's music are still these. It has always

1. Saint-Saëns is, of course, wrong. Beethoven's was by no means the only program symphony, or even the first. The idea is at least as old as the set of symphonies on Ovid's *Metamorphoses* (1785) by Karl Ditters von Dittersdorf (1739–99). [*Editor*]

† Copyright 1942 and renewed 1970 by Virgil Thomson. Quoted by permission of the copyright owner.

been admired and played, even when expensive to execute. Certain works are less frequently performed than others. The musical world, which has usually been in agreement about the master's best qualities no less than about his particular weaknesses, has always granted him world primacy in the art of instrumentation and profound orginality of dramatic expression, as well as a highly personal, an inimitable approach to the procedures of musical composition. The razor edge, moreover, of his mind has never been denied. He was terrifyingly articulate both as a composer and as a critic. Also, his *Treatise on Instrumentation* is considered as fundamental a contribution to musical knowledge as Rameau's and Fux's works on harmony or Sebastian Bach's *Art of Fugue*. If worldwide admiration, both lay and professional, and a profound influence on the technique of his art do not define "greatness" in a composer, then I give up.

That Berlioz's musical production is uneven in quality is of no importance. So is everybody else's. That a just balance between expression and virtuosity is less regularly achieved in them than in the works of his classical-minded predecessors is not surprising. He was, after all, a Romantic; and the aim of all the Romantics was to produce a new kind of intensity by upsetting the classical ideal of a just balance between expression and virtuosity. They all overstepped the classic bounds of taste. Liszt's music is overrhetorical. Wagner's is full of Germanic jingo and shameless in its exploitation of his own and his audience's erotic instincts. Schumann's is boisterous, Mendelssohn's stuffy, Brahms's timid and overrespectful of the past. Even Verdi, the purest of them all, made sometimes such pure theater that all sane sense of plot and character disappears. Only Chopin, in the whole nineteenth century, wrote music regularly, habitually according to an æsthetic that would not have shocked Mozart or Handel.

In any age, moreover, the work of the most original creators is the least even of all in quality. Perhaps "greatness" is a quality that precludes originality. In that case, respect for it is merely a worship of power and of the status quo and should be discouraged. One of the surest markings of high quality in art is the existence side by side of undeniable and universally acceptable beauty with elements that never cease to surprise. If this latter quality is absent the work is no longer alive. If it is too constantly present the work gets put away on a shelf eventually for reference use only. The music of Hector Berlioz is neither dead nor buried. Much of it is as alive and beautiful as anybody's. * * *

AARON COPLAND

Berlioz Today †

Aaron Copland (1900–) offers a composer's explanation for the recent revival of interest in Berlioz's music. The article appeared in 1960.

Berlioz is the archetype of artist who needs periodic reappraisal by each epoch. His own period couldn't possibly have seen him as we do. To his own time Berlioz was an intransigent radical; to us he seems, at times, almost quaint. Wystan Auden once wrote: "Whoever wants to know the nineteenth century must know Berlioz." True enough, he was an embodiment of his time, and because of that I can't think of another composer of the past century I should have more wanted to meet. And yet, enmeshed in his personality are stylistic throwbacks to an earlier time; these tend to temper and equivocate the impression he makes of the typical nineteenth-century artist.

His biographer, Jacques Barzun, claims that one rarely finds a discussion of Berlioz "which does not very quickly lose itself in biographical detail." Berlioz is himself partly responsible for this because he wrote so engagingly about his life. Moreover, there is the fabulous life itself: the tireless activity as composer, critic, and conductor; the success story of the country doctor's son who arrives unknown in the big city (Paris) to study music and ends up, after several tries, with the Prix de Rome; the distracted and distracting love affairs; the indebtedness due to the hiring of large orchestras to introduce his works; the fights, the friends (Chopin, Liszt, De Vigny, Hugo), the triumphal trips abroad, the articles in the *Journal des Débats*, the *Mémoires*, and the bitter experiences of his last years. No wonder that in the midst of all this the music itself is sometimes lost sight of.

Admirers and detractors alike recognize that we are living in a period of Berlioz revival. Formerly his reputation rested upon a few

† "Berlioz Today," in *Copland on Music* by Aaron Copland, New York. Copyright 1960 by Aaron Copland. Reprinted by permission of Doubleday & Company, Inc., and André Deutsch, Ltd.

works that remained in the orchestral repertoire: principally the *Symphonie Fantastique* and some of the overtures. Then came repeated hearings of *Harold in Italy*, *Romeo and Juliet*, and the *Damnation of Faust*. Recordings have made *L'Enfance du Christ* and *The Trojans* familiar; even the *Nuits d'Été* are now sung. Perhaps before long we may hope to hear unknown works like the *Song of the Railroads* (1846) or *Sara the Bather* (1834).[1]

What explains this recent concern with the Berlioz *oeuvre*? My own theory is that something about his music strikes us as curiously right for our own time. There is something about the quality of emotion in his music—the feeling of romanticism classically controlled—that reflects one aspect of present-day sensibility. This is allied with another startling quality: his ability to appear at one and the same time both remote in time and then suddenly amazingly contemporary. Berlioz possessed a Stendhalian capacity for projecting himself into the future, as if he had premonitions of the path music was to take. By comparison, Wagner, in spite of all the hoopla surrounding his "music of the future," was really occupied with the task of creating the music of his own period. And yet, by the irony of musical history, Berlioz must have seemed old-fashioned to Wagner by the 1860's.

By the end of the century, however, it was clear that the French composer had left a strong imprint on the composers who followed after him. A study of *Harold in Italy* will uncover reminders of the work of at least a dozen late-nineteenth-century composers—Strauss, Mahler, Moussorgsky, Rimsky-Korsakoff, Grieg, Smetana, Verdi, Tchaikovsky, Saint-Saëns, Franck, Fauré. (Nor should we forget the impact he had on his own contemporaries, Liszt and Wagner.) How original it was in 1834 to give the role of protagonist to a solo instrument—in this case a viola—and create, not a concerto for the instrument, but a kind of obbligato role for which I can think of no precedent. The line from *Harold* to *Don Quixote* as Strauss drew him is unmistakable. The second movement of *Harold in Italy* has striking similarities to the monastic cell music in *Boris Godounoff*, with all of Moussorgsky's powers of suggestibility. Indeed, the history of nineteenth-century Russian music is unthinkable without Berlioz. Stravinsky says that he was brought up on his music, that it was played in the St. Petersburg of his student years as much as it has ever been played anywhere. Even the Berlioz songs, now comparatively neglected, were models for Massenet and Fauré to emulate. Nor is it fanciful to

---

1. Recordings released during 1969, the centennial of Berlioz's death, have filled in some of these gaps. [*Editor*]

imagine a suggestion of the later Schönberg in the eight-note chromatic theme that introduces the "Evocation" scene from the *Damnation of Faust*.

When I was a student, Berlioz was spoken of as if he were a kind of Beethoven *manqué*. This attempted analogy missed the point: Beethoven's nature was profoundly dramatic, of course, but the essence of Berlioz is that of the *theatrical* personality. I once tried to define this difference in relation to Mahler—who, by the way, bears a distinct resemblance to Berlioz in more than one respect—by saying that "the difference between Beethoven and Mahler is the difference between watching a great man walk down the street and watching a great actor act the part of a great man walking down the street." Berlioz himself touched on this difference in a letter to Wagner when he wrote: "I can only paint the moon when I see her image reflected at the bottom of a well." Robert Schumann must have had a similar idea when he said: "Berlioz, although he often ... conducts himself as madly as an Indian fakir, is quite as sincere as Haydn, when, with his modest air, he offers us a cherry blossom."[2] This inborn theatricality is a matter of temperament, not a matter of insincerity. It is allied with a love for the grand gesture, the naïve-heroic, the theatric-religious. (In recent times Honegger and Messiaen have continued this tradition in French music.) With Berlioz we seem to be watching the artist watching himself create rather than the creator in the act, pure and simple. This is different in kind from the picturesqueness of Beethoven's *Storm* in the *Pastoral Symphony*. Berlioz was undoubtedly influenced by Beethoven's evocation of nature, but his special genius led to the introduction of what amounted to a new genre—the theatric-symphonic—and there was nothing tentative about the introduction.

The fact that Berlioz was French rather than German makes much of the difference. Debussy said that Berlioz had no luck, that he was beyond the musical intelligence of his contemporaries and beyond the technical capacities of the performing musicians of his time. But think of the colossal bad luck to have been born in a century when music itself belonged, so to speak, to the Germans. There was something inherently tragic in his situation—the solitariness and the uniqueness of his appearance in France. Even the French themselves, as Henri Collet[3] makes clear, had considerable trouble in fitting Berlioz into their ideas of what a French composer should be. In a sense he belonged everywhere and nowhere, which may or may not explain the universality of his appeal. In

---

2. From an essay of 1836, *Die Preissymphonie*. [*Editor*]
3. Henri Collet (1885–1951), French music critic. [*Editor*]

spite of Berlioz's passionate regard for the music of Beethoven and Weber and Gluck, it is the non-German concept of his music that gives it much of its originality.

This can perhaps be most clearly observed in his writing for orchestra. Even his earliest critics admitted his brilliance as orchestrator. But they could hardly have guessed that a century later we would continue to be impressed by Berlioz's virtuoso handling of an orchestra. It is no exaggeration to say that Berlioz invented the modern orchestra. Up to his time most composers wrote for the orchestra as if it were an enlarged string quintet—none before him had envisaged the blending of orchestral instruments in such a way as to produce new combinations of sonorities. In Bach and Mozart a flute or a bassoon always sounds like a flute or a bassoon; with Berlioz they are given, along with their own special quality, a certain ambiguity of timbre that introduces an element of orchestral magic as a contemporary composer would understand it. The brilliance of his orchestration comes partly by way of his instinctual writing for the instruments in their most grateful registers and partly by way of his blending of instruments rather than merely keeping them out of each other's way. Add to this an incredible daring in forcing instrumentalists to play better than they knew they could play. He paid the price of his daring, no doubt, in hearing his music inadequately performed. But imagine the excitement of hearing in one's inner ear sonorities that had never before been set down on paper. It is the sheen and sparkle, the subtle calculation of these masterly scores that convince me that Berlioz was more, much more, than the starry-eyed romantic of the history books.

It is easy to point to specific examples of Berlioz's orchestral boldness. The use of the double-basses in four-part chordal pizzicati at the beginning of the *March to the Scaffold*; the writing for four timpani, also in chordal style, at the conclusion of the movement that precedes the *March*; the use of English horn and piccolo clarinet to typify pastoral and devilish sentiments respectively; the gossamer texture of *Queen Mab* with its impressionist harp and high antique cymbals; the subtle mixtures of low flutes with string tone at the beginning of the "Love Scene" from *Romeo*—all these and numerous other examples demonstrate Berlioz's uncanny instinct for the sound stuff of music.

Apart from his orchestral know-how there is hardly a phase of his music that has not been subjected to criticism. His harmonic sense is said to be faulty—that's the reproach most frequently heard—his structure too dependent on extramusical connotations, his melodic line disappointingly old-fashioned. These oft-repeated strictures are now due for revi-

sion. Any clumsiness in the handling of harmonic progressions should be viewed in the light of our extended notions of right and wrong in harmonic procedures. The Berlioz harmony admittedly is sometimes stiff and plain, but is it so awkward as to disturb one's over-all enjoyment? That always has seemed an exaggerated claim to me. His formal sense is unconventional—refreshingly so, I would say, for even when he lacks the inevitability of a Beethoven, one senses that he is finding his own solutions arrived at from his own premises. More often than not these are unexpected and surprising. The reproach concerning his melodic writing has some basis in fact, especially for the present-day listener. Berlioz depends upon the long-breathed line and the unconventional phrase length, to sustain interest, rather than the striking interval or pregnant motive. His loveliest melodies give off a certain daguerreotype charm, redolent of another day. This must have been true even at the time he penned them. Looked at from this angle, they lend his music a quite special *ambiance,* as if they came from a country not to be found on any map.

Let us concede, for the sake of argument, that the weaknesses are there. The fact remains that, whenever a composer is adjudged worthy to stand with the masters, a remarkable willingness to overlook what was formerly considered to be serious weaknesses is apparent. The weaknesses remain, but public opinion tacitly agrees to accept them for the sake of the good qualities—and I consider that public opinion does right. My prognostication is that we shall, in future, be hearing less and less of Berlioz's weaknesses and more and more of his strengths.

For I repeat that there is something strangely right about Berlioz for our time. The French historian Paul Landormy[4] put my meaning well when he wrote: "His art has an objective character by comparison with the subjectivity (intériorité) of a Beethoven or a Wagner. All the creatures that he created in his imagination detach themselves from him, take on independent life, even if they are only an image of himself. The Germans, on the contrary, have a tendency to fuse the entire universe with their interior life. Berlioz is essentially a Latin artist." It is the objective handling of romantic elements that makes Berlioz an especially sympathetic figure in our own time. That and our clear perception of his musical audacity. For he is clearly one of the boldest creators that ever practiced the art of musical composition.

4. Paul Landormy (1869–1943). The quotation is from his *Histoire de la musique,* 2nd rev. ed., Paris, 1946, p. 261. [*Editor*]

An aura of something larger than life-size hangs about his name. After hearing a Berlioz concert Heinrich Heine wrote: "Here is a wing-beat that reveals no ordinary songbird, it is a colossal nightingale, a lark as big as an eagle, such as must have existed in the primeval world." [5]

5. Berlioz himself approvingly cites this passage from Heine's *Lutetia.* See *Memoirs,* pp. 478–79. [*Editor*]

And in Brief

During a conversation with Claude Rostand, Darius Milhaud (1892–) concluded a discussion of Wagner by exclaiming:

"Whew! Give me some fresh air! I would give up all of Wagner for one page of Berlioz!"[1]

But the last word should go to Gioacchino Rossini (1792–1868) — somewhat doubtfully, to be sure, for, like all great wits, he was given credit for many spurious bon mots. He is said to have made the following remark while examining the score of the *Fantastic Symphony*:

"What a good thing that young man has never taken up music! He would certainly be very bad at it."

1. Darius Milhaud, *Entretiens avec Claude Rostand*, Paris, 1952, p. 61. Copyright 1952 by René Julliard. Translated and quoted by permission of the publisher.

Bibliography

Barzun, Jacques, *Berlioz and the Romantic Century*, 2 vols., Boston, 1950; 3rd ed., New York, 1969. The fullest account in English of Berlioz's life and works. It contains an unusually complete and detailed bibliography.
———— *Berlioz and His Century*, New York, 1956. A second edition of the above, considerably abridged.
Berlioz, Hector, *Grand traité d'instrumentation et d'orchestration modernes*, Paris, [1843]. The most useful version of this work (to which Berlioz actually gave an opus number, 10) is the German translation of the revised edition (1855) by Alfred Dörffel, in turn revised and enlarged by Richard Strauss; as *Instrumentationslehre* it was published by Peters, Leipzig, 1905. An English translation by Theodore Front of the Berlioz-Strauss was published as *Treatise on Instrumentation*, New York, 1948.
———— *Lettres intimes*, Paris, 1882. Several volumes of Berlioz's correspondence have been published. This one contains letters relating to the composition of the *Fantastic Symphony*. Some of these are translated by Humphrey Searle in *Hector Berlioz, a Selection from His Letters*, London, 1966.
———— *Memoirs of Hector Berlioz*, transl. by David Cairns, New York, 1969. An excellent version of a fascinating autobiography.
Boschot, Adolphe, *Hector Berlioz*, 3 vols. (I, *La Jeunesse d'un romantique*; II: *Un Romantique sous Louis-Philippe*; III, *Le Crépuscule d'un romantique*), Paris, 1906–13; revised ed., 1946–50. Accepted for many years as the definitive biography, this work is actually full of distortions due to the basic lack of sympathy of the author with his subject.
——— *Une Vie romantique, Hector Berlioz*, Paris, 1919; revised ed., 1939. An abridgement of the above in one volume.
Cone, Edward T., "Inside the Saint's Head: The Music of Berlioz," in *Musical Newsletter*, I/3 (1971), 3–12; I/4 (1971), 11–20; and II/1 (1972), 19–22.
Hopkinson, Cecil, *A Bibliography of the Works of Hector Berlioz, 1803–69*, Edinburgh, 1951.
Macdonald, Hugh, *Berlioz Orchestral Music*, London, 1969.
Primmer, Brian, *The Berlioz Style*, London, 1973.
Temperley, Nicholas, editor, *Hector Berlioz, New Edition of the Complete Works*, XVI, *Symphonie fantastique*, Kassel, Basel, Tours, London, 1972.
———— "The *Symphonie fantastique* and Its Program," in *The Musical Quarterly*, LVII/4 (1971), 593–608.
Tiersot, Julien, *Berlioz et la société de son temps*, Paris, 1904.

———— "The Berlioz of the Fantastic Symphony," in *The Musical Quarterly*, XIX 3 (1933), 303–17.

———— "Berlioziana," a series of articles published in the French magazine *Le Ménestrel*, 1904–06. Those dealing with the *Fantastic Symphony* are in the issues of June 26 to July 10, 1904, and May 20 to Aug. 5, 1906.

Turner, W. J., *Berlioz, the Man and His Work*, London, 1935.

Wotton, Tom S., *Berlioz: Four Works*, London, 1929. In the *Musical Pilgrim* series. It contains a discussion of the *Fantastic Symphony*.

———— *Hector Berlioz*, London, 1935.